BAC-SI

A Doctor Remembers Vietnam

Phong Dien village office hours.

BAC-SI

A Doctor Remembers Vietnam

by Peter Caldwell, M.D.

Taote Publishing • Honolulu, Hawaii

Taote Publishing
P.O. Box 22660
Honolulu, Hawaii 96823

Photographs by the author
Illustrations by Marcia Prins

Publisher's Cataloging in Publication Data

Library of Congress Catalog Card Number: 90-90086

ISBN 0-9626124-0-5

Printed in the United States of America

Author's Note

Twenty-four years ago I sat in a Boeing 707 and watched the Da Nang airfield slide away past the window for the last time. Much to my surprise, that year in Vietnam as a Navy physician with the Marine Corps had turned out to be one of the most worthwhile and educational of my life. As with all of us who were "down South" in one way or the other, I find my memories remain vivid and easily recalled. As far as any serious writing attempts about my experiences, I'd been content most of the time to be an interested reader of other accounts of the war. Such an approach was certainly much easier for those of us who didn't shine in college English.

However, in recent years, Hollywood has become much more interested in Vietnam, and there has been a flurry of activity on the literary scene as well. A friend of mine, after finishing one particular book, commented to me that now he thought he really had a good feel for what Vietnam was really like. Reading the same pages, I found myself thinking—no, there was a lot more to it than that. But, after all, I couldn't expect the infantryman's or correspondent's perspective to match my own. Vietnam experiences varied considerably, from the relatively plush living conditions of being in "the rear with the gear" to the worst kind of miserable existence in the field. As medical officers we were not taken seriously as military men, which was certainly appropriate. As my infantry battalion commander used to say, the most dangerous person to be around in Vietnam was a medical officer with a .45 (we were all required to carry a .45 caliber pistol, being generic officers). But our medical status presented us with unusual opportunities to enter the world of the Vietnamese civilian population and see another side of the war.

Descriptions of Marine field operations and discussion of military strategy and its effectiveness have not received much attention throughout this account. Likewise I have not intended to dwell on the specifics of our care of casualties. Suffice it to say that compared to past wars, our medical treatment was significantly upgraded by the extensive use of helicopters to provide fast access to definitive surgical therapy. My focus is on filling in the gaps in the landscape of the Vietnam war apart from tense jungle patrols, chaotic firefights, and stark combat bases. This material is based on a daily journal. Names have been changed to protect the privacy of the individuals involved.

Here then are some additional and different glimpses of the people and the country that were all an integral part of I Corps, Republic of Vietnam, in 1966-1967, from the viewpoint of a fortunate non combatant.

Peter Caldwell, M.D.
Honolulu, Hawaii
March 1991

Acknowledgments

Special thanks to Priit Vesilind for copy editing, and to Marcia Prins for illustrations and layout. Thanks also to Olga Caldwell, Kimie Hirabayashi M.D., and David Miller for proofreading, and to Lynne Meyer of MacTypeNet for general guidance, typesetting, and patience with revision after revision. In addition, I would like to thank my mother, Mary E. Caldwell, for encouraging me to keep a journal during my year in Vietnam and subsequently to do something with the material.

Contents

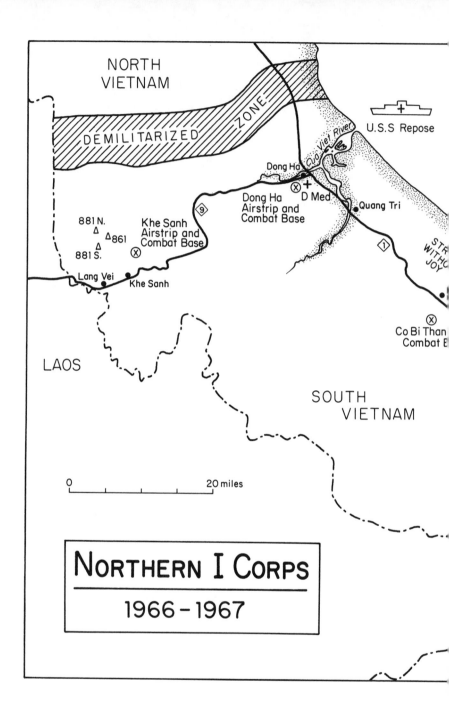

NORTH
VIETNAM

DEMILITARIZED ZONE

U.S.S Repose

Cua Viet River

Dong Ha

D Med

Dong Ha
Airstrip and
Combat Base

Quang Tri

881 N.
861
881 S.

Khe Sanh
Airstrip and
Combat Base

Lang Vei

Khe Sanh

STR
WITH
JOY

Co Bi Than
Combat B

LAOS

SOUTH
VIETNAM

0   20 miles

NORTHERN I CORPS

1966 – 1967

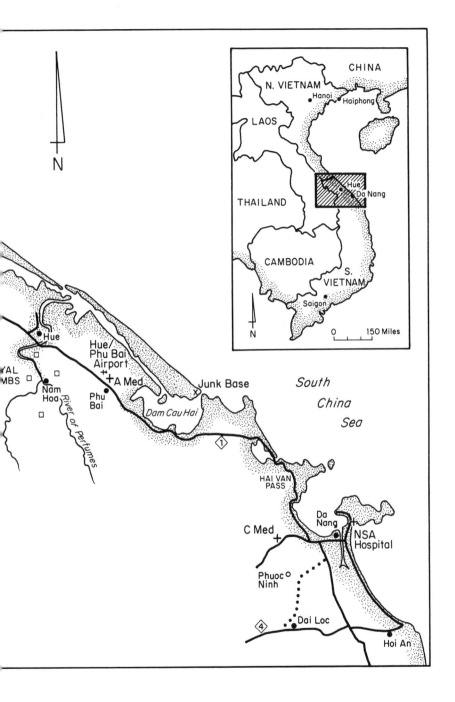

Babysitters, Dai Loc.

CHAPTER ONE

Instant
Grunt

The queen of spades made her inevitable appearance. "Chief," exclaimed the chaplain, "let me introduce you to my favorite lady—the one and and only Black Queen!" The chaplain was on a roll during this particular evening's hotly contested game of hearts at the battalion aid station, and he was not one to let that fact go unnoticed.

"I am no match for mortal men—bring me giants !" he roared as the other three groaned.

The night was relatively quiet, other than the occasional distant boom of artillery fire and "Winchester Cathedral" coming from a tape recorder in the next tent. My gaze shifted from the card game to the memo I held in my hand addressed to the battalion surgeon, 2nd Battalion, 4th Marines. Battalion surgeon—it sounded fairly impressive, but actually we were on the low end of the totem pole in the medical hierarchy in Vietnam. Most of us were just out of internship and very few were actually surgeons. The road from civilian life to battalion surgeon status was often quite a short one. The Marine Corps might build men but they acquired their physicians made to order, courtesy of the U.S. Navy. My thoughts drifted back to the time about nine months ago when I was standing in the lobby of King County Hospital in Seattle and staring at a nearly unintelligible piece of paper full of abbreviations and mumbo-jumbo that made medical jargon look like an elementary school reader. However, my eyes fastened primarily on the section that read: ...proceed Camp Pendleton California and report CO FMSS Marine Corps Base on 8 July...

Now wait a minute—I thought I signed up with the Navy. There must be some mistake. Proving the value of eight years of higher education, I had failed to appreciate the fact that the Marine Corps and U.S. Navy were really one and the same when it came to the medical department. In 1966 you really didn't have any alternative when it came to military service, other than enlist out of internship into the branch of service of your choice or apply for deferment for specialty training with active duty to follow. As a result, a number of us who were undecided about future specialty plans could be found marching down to the local recruiting office in a burst of not-so-patriotic fervor.

The Navy—romance of the high seas, exotic ports of call. That didn't sound all that bad. But the Marines? Guadalcanal? Sands of Iwo Jima? That was not what I had in mind at all.

At Camp Pendleton one month later, it turned out that the Marines weren't figuring in the plans of quite a few of the 200-odd, somewhat bewildered and recalcitrant doctors and dentists who were welcomed aboard. Some were in a more undesirable situation than I was because they were only halfway through their residencies. For those who were not single, the year away looked even worse. The atmosphere was charged with a definite lack of enthusiasm. But the Corps didn't discourage easily, and we were off to the classroom to be deluged with lectures on the history and organization of the Marine Corps, gung-ho movies, and practical matters somehow overlooked in medical school such as field stripping an M14 rifle, etc. We were halfway expecting John Wayne himself to show up in full battle gear.

Being an instant officer had other aspects, some of which were not too welcome, especially when every grunt around knew full well that despite our rank we were greener than our brand new fatigues, or "utilities" in Marine Corpsese. It was like being a freshman in college all over again and avoiding upper classmen on campus for fear of harassment. Only at Camp Pendleton it was commonplace in those early days to plan your route carefully to avoid contact with regular line officers or especially enlisted men. Why? It was the little matter of the salute. However there was no escape, and inevitably some lance corporal would walk by with a sharp and snappy USMC elite salute and a brisk "Good Morning, Sir!" accompanied by just a trace of a snicker. He would be answered by a mumble and an awkward excuse for a salute that looked like a man scratching his forehead with his arthritic arm.

The classroom, though, was just the beginning of our crash indoctrination. We were offered an opportunity to shine in all the traditional Marine activities. The obstacle course for example, gave a number of the not-so-physically gifted among us a chance to provide a few laughs for our instructors with some very rusty or relative lack of athletic skills. Then there was our first exercise in map and compass reading. We were halfway through our problem for the day, and it was time for chow—our first crack at the famous C-rations.

We were gathered in a little tree-shaded draw which served as an outdoor classroom as a truck pulled up with boxes of "Cees" and large coolers of water. My friend, Sandy Foreman, a skinny former New York City hospital intern with a definite distaste for the military, got at the head of the line and grabbed a couple of boxes off the stack, tossing one to me.

"I hope you picked a good one, " I said, as we looked around for a place to enjoy our feast.

"How about over there by that pipe?" I suggested. "A little sun so you can make use of your hard-core Marine sunglasses." We ended up sitting next to a ten-inch diameter pipe standing about 2 1/2 feet above the ground, covered on the top with wire mesh. A vent for some underground storage bunker? Who knows? Time to see what gourmet items we had selected.

"Ham and lima beans," exclaimed Sandy. "You got to be kidding me."

About then a corporal came up to the two of us, who were pretty much alone at that point. He saluted, smiling a little, and said, "Begging your pardon, sir, but are you officers aware that you are sitting next to the piss tube?"

Glad that the noonday sun might somehow have hidden the reddening of my face, I tried to reply nonchalantly, "No problem corporal. We were just looking for a place with some sun."

As we cleared the area in record time, we began to notice the presence of a familiar odor. "Sandy! What's wrong with you, man! You've got the map. Why didn't you tell me we were sitting next to a piss tube?"

Sandy rolled his eyes and shook his head: "To think I could have signed up for the Air Force." The next day we got our regular classroom lectures about Marine Corps sanitation practices, including trench latrines, 4-holers, and yes, a little too late, piss tubes.

The rifle range provided some moments also. The targets were supposed to be a mere 200 yards away but half a mile seemed to be more realistic. As I assumed the regulation prone position, trying to get semi-comfortable, I was thinking that nothing short of a guided-missile round would get me a hit on that distant target. For those in our group with firearm or hunting background, it wasn't that strange, but for me, having never used any weapon more potent than a water pistol, it was quite a novel experience. Trying to remember how to use the rifle's sights produced the usual classroom blur, and I couldn't figure out which eye to use. Oh well, I thought, it probably wouldn't make any difference anyway. The order came to commence firing, and the M14 recoiled violently as I watched my first round plow into a low ridge of dirt about 25 yards away. I noticed down the line other puffs of dirt even closer than my first effort. I was beginning to develop a little more respect for those sharpshooter and expert medals worn by many Marines. Ears ringing, we left the range as a group that had probably eclipsed all existing records for total futility. Watch out VC, don't mess with the medical officers.

Close-order drill. Picture those precise USMC units you see at parades and football games. Then replace that image with a MAD magazine platoon of troops so uncoordinated that a command for left face usually resulted in assorted individuals facing the opposite direction. There were a few probably deliberately trying to foil the suffering drill instructor, who had the distinctly distasteful task of dealing with a contingent of uninspired and even surly medical officers. "I would appreciate it if you would turn right when I say turn right—SIR!" How badly he must have wanted to call us scumbags or numbnuts, but what could a staff sergeant do with a bunch of worthless lieutenants anyway?

Also on the program was a stroll through the mine and booby trap course. We saw all varieties of trip-wired grenades and mines including "Bouncing Bettys," which were designed to spring up and explode at waist level. Taking advantage of local materials were medieval inventions like a huge sod ball with imbedded sharp bamboo stakes, poised to swing down into the trail. There were even fiendish creations with a one-two punch—a small disguised pit with a nail in a plank in the bottom so that when the victim instinctively withdrew his foot from the spike, a grenade would be triggered. Even in the face of these sinister devices, the reality of Vietnam still seemed far away, and the general atmosphere was that of a large Boy Scout camp—a break from the usual medical routine.

The picture began to come into more sobering focus when we left the cool comfort of our 707 and stepped out into the sweltering, oppressive heat of Okinawa's Kadena Air Base, where you seemed to knock water out of the air with each step. After a few days layover in Okinawa, we were back again at Kadena waiting to board our Da Nang-bound aircraft.

However, we had a last-minute two-hour reprieve due to engine trouble, as our plane supposedly had recently taken some .50 caliber rounds through one engine on a recent trip "down South." Hmmmm.

A short time later we were approaching our final destination—scattered dark clouds, brooding green mountains rising inland from the coastal plains with sheets of rain to the south, scattered houses and huts, the occasional checkerboard of rice paddies, and then a muddy brown river twisting like an evil snake with a crumpled and broken bridge in the middle. War? You'd think we were landing in Vietnam, and then suddenly we were—Da Nang airfield. The blur rushing by slowed to reveal planes of all kinds. There were sleek, camouflaged F4 Phantoms, single-engine reconnaissance planes, and also a sight soon to be part of almost every day—Marine helicopters.

In addition, there were sandbagged gun emplacements, radar installations, storage buildings and hangars, all with a thrown-together appearance and disorganization different from any other airport I had ever seen. Then we heard a facetious, "Welcome to the Republic of Vietnam," from our friendly steward, safe in the knowledge he would soon be leaving.

We stepped off the plane in a slow drizzle of warm rain and walked over towards a broken-down bus which was to take us to the "terminal." On the way we passed a group of Marines in rumpled khakis waiting with their sea bags. They watched us parade by with apparently amused half-smiles. You could read their minds with ease: Those poor bastards— twelve months to go. And of course we were among the relatively fortunate men who were in the non-combatant category. You could imagine the feeling of a 19-year-old Marine PFC rifleman in the same position.

Some of our colleagues who were destined for the 1st Marine Division were soon on their way to Chu Lai on an old transport plane belonging to "Trans Paddy Airways." The rest of us piled into trucks for a trip to Charlie Med, headquarters for the 3rd Marine Division's Medical Battalion.

Sandy and I sat together, gazing disconsolately at the surroundings with the same unspoken thought—what in the world are we doing in this place? The road was rear-axle deep in thick, red mud, and we jolted along looking at rows of tents pitched on wooden frames with at least a floor, rolls of surrounding barbed wire, and sandbagged bunkers. The romance was definitely over. Here was our home for the next year, I was thinking as we rolled through Dogpatch. So aptly named was this dirty village that had grown up near the airfield. It was pure squalor in a half shell with dirty children, scrawny dogs, and leering prostitutes. The street and its inhabitants looked like a great culture media for every known parasitic and infectious disease.

Entering C-Med as our gloomy moods became submerged in the early evening darkness, we passed a helicopter holding area, Quonset huts and "hardbacks" (screened wooden framed structures with corrugated tin roofs). There were also some familiar landmarks from FMSS days—the house with the 4-holes, except in this case it was called the "Medical Library." We were deposited in front of a larger hardback with a battered sign lit by two bare bulbs—The Perimeter Club—the local officer's hangout. At this point, I was feeling very conspicuous in my new utilities, and as I jumped out of the truck, I was halfway hoping for a good slip in the mud to acquire some resemblance to the hard-bitten veterans we certainly were not.

After a trip down the chow line, we spent the rest of the evening listening to war stories from our hosts, many of whom were soon-to-depart "short-timers" who carried on with all the flair of career foreign legionnaires. We learned that those with their residency training completed would spend their tours in the relative comfort and security of a field hospital like C-Med. General medical officers, on the other hand, could look forward to a year that included some time at a field hospital doing triage and sick call work, possibly two months at a rear-echelon unit and the remainder with the grunts, as each infantry battalion rated two medical officers. Our thoughts of what life in RVN was going to be like were suddenly interrupted by a tremendous explosion. Mortared already in the first night? There were a lot of wide-eyed new doctors stopped in mid-sentence looking for a place to hide. The veterans didn't even blink, informing us calmly that some Vietnamese were blasting a rock quarry nearby. Somewhat reassuring was the word that C-Med hadn't taken any incoming rounds for over six months, and usually the only event disturbing your sleep was the loud wap-wap-wap of helicopters landing at night.

Near my cot on that first night was someone's nearly completed short-timer's calendar. This important document had a shapely girl covered with 100 squares, with each blackened square representing one day closer to the magic flight date home, the last few days' squares being located in strategic places. So why look at that calendar with such envy, I thought, as I tried to get comfortable on my rickety, creaking bed. After all, I only had 364 days to go.

Six months later, from the vantage point of a Vietnam-wise veteran, that initial troubled night was years back. It seemed as though I'd been here so long already, not that time was dragging so much as one might expect, but actually because so many things had happened: The first six weeks at A-Med, a smaller field hospital south of Hue; then to the battalion at Dong Ha near the DMZ, meeting the horrendous trauma of war head on; the frustrations and rewards of trying to provide semi-modern medical care for Vietnamese civilians with old fashioned methods; the countless trips to country hamlets, villages, orphanages, and dispensaries; some memorable helicopter rides; the citadel in Hue and the royal tombs. The list could go on and on, and I had only come halfway so far. Now nearing the end of one month at Dai Loc, 15 miles south of Da Nang, I was beginning to recognize some new feelings, in particular one of real involvement with the people of the village and some of the outlying hamlets.

Last week, a beefy, rednecked Marine NCO had described me as a "gook lover" because he and one of his men had to spend a little time waiting in the BAS while I first debrided an old Vietnamese woman's fragment wound. I told him I was not a Marine doctor, but a doctor in the Marines and that meant the occasional wounded Vietnamese brought to us took priority over flat feet or a case of the usual post R & R infectious disease. Cooling down from that outburst, I realized that I couldn't really expect that the average grunt, who at times perhaps had received sniper fire from a supposedly friendly hamlet or had even watched a buddy get blown to pieces by a mine, would have much sympathy for my viewpoint or empathy with the Vietnamese. Unlike the world of the rifleman out in the "weeds" on a patrol, I was not dealing with impassive treacherous civilians or suspicious "gooks." I was seeing a different side of war, i.e. the effects of an endless conflict on simple, hardworking country people who were trying to adjust and endure in spite of the all-too-frequent tragic disruptions. After working and laughing with them, trying to cure their mysterious fevers and unravel their vague complaints, feeling the warmth of their appreciation for the most minor service, and suffering along with them through the consequences of VC terrorism or an errant artillery round, I had reached the point where I knew there might be sadness and mixed feelings when departure time arrived.

"Hey, Doc-san, come to the party," came the chaplain's voice from a distance. "Where have you been when I needed you to protect me from these sharks?"

With my most serious and contemplative look, I replied slowly, "You know, to tell you the truth, I've been thinking about going to seminary when I get out of here."

"Corpsman," he shouted, "come take this man's temperature. I think I've got a heat casualty."

"Tell him sick call is at 0900 in the morning," came a voice from the table.

"Shut up and deal the f—— cards, McClosky." There was a brief silence followed by, "Oh excuse me, padre." The chaplain smiled and headed for the door.

CHAPTER TWO

Mai's First Smile

Our jeep bounced along the dusty rutted road, a narrow brown ribbon unwinding through the brilliant green of spring growth in the rice paddies. I had plans to drop off some additional supplies at CAP 3-1, where recently the corpsman had been doing a brisk sick-call business. Along with the usual complement of a squad of Marines and local Vietnamese militiamen, this particular CAP or combined action platoon, had a corpsman named Elwood who never failed to amaze all of us with his dedication and commitment. It wasn't even the idealism of a new man on the job either, as he was a relative short-timer and talking extension. Speaking Vietnamese with a North Carolina accent, he fulfilled his role better than any rear-area civil affairs paper shuffler ever would have imagined. In addition to getting high marks in its hamlet security and medical function, his unit had also helped with some village school repairs and initiated an irrigation project. The daily Saigon "Jive at Five" sessions would do well to include some accounts of accomplishments of people like Elwood instead of the usual here-we-go-again operational reports.

As we rounded a curve and approached the bridge just past La Chau hamlet, I turned to Sam Topping, our battalion civil affairs officer, and commented that the road ahead seemed a little congested. The reason was soon apparent. The Viet Cong, affectionately known as Victor Charlie, had once again altered our plans. Charred and broken remnants of the recently rebuilt wooden bridge testified to the latest nocturnal activity of the local Viet Cong. Some Vietnamese were already moving in to clear the debris and carry off some of the smaller pieces for firewood. The Dai

Loc "expressway" would once again be closed to commuter traffic. We turned around in frustration and decided instead to pay a visit to CAP 3-3, about one kilometer to the south, where the corpsman had reported finding a little girl with a bad cleft lip and palate. I was all too well acquainted with the unbelievable destructive effects of modern weapons on the human body. A chance to help with something besides the disastrous trauma of war was welcomed. At the NSA hospital in Da Nang, elective surgery for civilians was available when time permitted, and we had been on the lookout for prospective patients, especially children with such defects.

Narrowly missing a pig on the way in, we rattled through the sand-bagged enclosure into the courtyard of the concrete block and tin-roofed building which served as the CAP's command post. Morris, the corpsman, was in the back demonstrating the magic of a Polaroid camera to a group of wide-eyed village kids. I interrupted the show to ask him about the girl. He sent one of the Marines, a graduate of a Vietnamese language school, and two PFs off across the paddies to Phuoc Ninh, the hamlet where she was supposed to live.

Soon they returned accompanied by the girl and her father. She was definitely not the usual inquisitive, chattering eight-year-old, and for good reason: short black hair framed a sorrowful face disfigured by a severe cleft lip and palate. She stood stoically by her father's side, dressed in faded and shabby, but surprisingly clean clothes. Taking a closer look, the defects were as bad as Morris had said, maybe even worse. I tried some of my not-so-fluent Vietnamese, but I knew before I started that there was no way I would get a response from her. I sure couldn't try the Polaroid either. It turned out that her name was Le Thi Mai, and by the sad, woeful look in her large brown eyes, it was pretty clear that she had endured more than her fair share of painful teasing because of her defect. Back in the "World", as the U.S.A. was commonly referred to in Vietnam, such an abnormality would have been bad enough, but here it was simply a question of fatalistic acceptance, as plastic surgery was not in the picture at all. In fact, in rural Vietnam, a *bac-si* (physician) of any kind was not in the picture.

Through the CAP interpreter, I explained to her father about the possibility of corrective surgery at our hospital in Da Nang, but he couldn't seem to believe that such a procedure was available for Vietnamese. Finally, after more discussion and some hesitation on his part, he appeared to agree to the operation, and I told him that we would work on the arrangements.

"She might be back, she might not," said Morris as we watched them head back toward Phuoc Ninh. "They're good people in that village. If only the Viet Cong would leave them the hell alone. Two weeks ago Charlie came in at night to remind them to be more cooperative. They lobbed grenades into the hamlet chief's house, killing him, his wife, and their three children. Then there was a brief firefight with one PF killed and three wounded. One VC got zapped, and they took the son of a bitch and hung him by his feet where people in the village took turns stabbing the body until we finally went in and talked them into letting us cut it down. Can't say as I really blame them."

I asked Morris how well he knew Mai's father. "He seems pretty squared away," Morris answered "and I really think he trusts us. You can bet he'll hear stories about what happens to Vietnamese children who go off with Americans. But I think they'll show, I really do."

Driving back to Dai Loc we stopped for some pictures along the road. During this time of the afternoon, with the sun slanting across the paddies and dying out in the shadowy ravines between purple and green mountains to the west, it was beautiful and very tranquil. What a little peace would do for this country! Sam, ever on the lookout for a tourist shot, decided he wanted a picture of himself carrying a typical farmer's load. Conveniently, a boy of about 12 or 13 was passing by with a load of firewood in wicker baskets hanging from the ubiquitous carrying pole. After taking his picture, we succeeded in convincing him to allow Topping to give it a try. Smiling confidently, six-footer Sam hoisted pole and baskets up on his shoulder. I squeezed the shutter, catching his somewhat puzzled look as he said, "Wow, this stuff is heavier than it looks." Then he stepped off the road for "effect" he said, and in a few seconds he was flat on his butt in the adjoining paddy while the photographer and the original subject were breaking up over the nimble-footed display.

"Hold it, Grace," I said while trying to keep the camera steady.

"Anything for a good picture," he muttered, pulling himself out of the soft red goo like a prehistoric creature emerging from the La Brea tar pits.

"Numbah 10," laughed the boy, shaking his head as he picked up his load with practiced ease and walked off.

A few sights along the road as we continued the rest of the way: Nobody was too old or too young to carry something. One old woman had a pig in a basket on each end of her carrying pole. Two men were struggling with a huge water pot which looked too heavy to lift, let alone haul down the road. A contingent of PFs were coming back from patrol, some carrying cooking pots along with carbines. One music lover had his portable radio comfortably draped over his shoulder, resting on a couple of grenades. Passing a couple of small resettlement refugee villages, we saw the usual large numbers of children. The very young, one to three years old, were usually standing wide-eyed and staring in front of a hut. No diaper problems here; the pants didn't come on until the plumbing was in working order. Boys in the six-to-ten age group, wearing raggedy shirts and shorts and often a battered jungle hat, ran alongside the jeep, with comments ranging from, "Hey, Marine, you numbah One," to "Chop-chop," to "Ceegarette?" Girls of the same age were frequently baby-sitters carrying a younger sister or brother astride one hip.

And of course there were grim reminders of the war—not just conventional warfare, but too often your basic terrorist atrocities as practiced by the noble patriots of the National Liberation Front. The twisted remains of a bus lay off the road. Several weeks ago it was disintegrated by a massive hand-detonated land mine which was placed under a metal culvert to avoid detection by the mine sweepers. The bus was blown completely off the road with sickening results: 14 killed and 33 others badly wounded. Golf company's CP was on a hill nearby, and John Russell, one of the corpsmen, was among the first on the scene. He told me it was the worst he'd ever seen in 10 months in in-country, with the majority of the passengers being old people, women and children. How could they possibly do that to their own people?

Back at our hillside CP along the Song Vu River, I was holding forth after dinner out along the perimeter wire fronting the river bend with the gang of kids who were now regulars at that spot. They gathered at dusk and there was always banter back and forth as they tried out their English, and I entertained them with my best Vietnamese. The most outgoing, outgoing, high-spirited of the group was a brash ten-year-old boy named Johnny. There was also one little girl of about seven named Ly, with an irresistible smile, who always ended up with more than her share of the mess tent goodies that I brought with me. "Honcho, Honcho *Bac-si*," they would yell when they saw me coming. I passed out oranges and cookies, but first they had to say the English words. How fast they learned, but quickly a local vocabulary developed, even rhymes. "Hey, Doc, give me *bom* (apple)," said one little boy over and over. Ly, taking an orange, announced, "Thank you, *Dai-uy Bac-si*, I souvenir you banana," as she offered one across the wire. Watching Ly, I thought about sad Mai at Phuoc Ninh. Could we manage to get her smiling and laughing like these kids?

All that was required was a wave or wink, and you had a new friend among these country children whose natural curiosity and adaptability served them well in their wartime environment. Even the most hard-core grunt could be won over by kids who seemed to materialize at almost every stop. Sick-calls in the country here would guarantee not only many small patients but also numerous young spectators. Small ones would sometimes boldly dash up just to touch the tall strange *bac-si* and then run off giggling. You became a Pied Piper at times, and if you made the mistake of giving one child a ride on your shoulder, you had to be ready for equal time for many more. "Marine numbah 1. Ho Chi Minh numbah 10," they would say, but yet we would hear about Vietnamese children in some areas selling Marines soda laced with ground glass. Surely not in Dai Loc, but there was always that lingering uncertainty about every harmless-appearing situation.

That night around midnight, all hell broke loose in the compound. The whole perimeter seemed to be under fire. Bursts of automatic fire, tracers and flares were everywhere. Our tent door saw a fast parade of green undershort-clad figures heading for the nearest bunker, but at least no incoming rounds close by yet. Suddenly we realized what was going on. It was Tet (Vietnamese New Year), and our South Vietnamese allies were simply doing some celebrating. It would have been nice to get a little forewarning.

There were a few near misses. Close to the battalion aid station, a 60 mm mortar illumination round dud crashed through a tent and into somebody's unoccupied rack. "I spent an hour on my belly in the Chapel," fumed the chaplain describing many apparent close rounds. Oh well, *Chuc Mung Nam Moi!* (Happy New Year!)

The following day I got on the radio to the NSA hospital in Da Nang and set it up for Mai whenever they next had some time available in the operating room. Two weeks later, while the battalion was involved in Operation Cleveland, Morris was able to take Mai into Da Nang on a resupply run. Later he told us that there were only a few tears, and she seemed to be quite resigned to her fate. Despite the presence of other Vietnamese in the small civilian ward at NSA, I could imagine that the strange surroundings must have been far from comforting to a little girl whose previous travels had been limited to the next hamlet. Also making Mai's situation unusual was the fact that, in Vietnam, hospitalization was a family affair, and the common routine was for what seemed like the entire family to move in with the patient and set up housekeeping. This particular cultural practice didn't really seem to contribute much to our Western concepts of good medical care, and needless to say, was not standard practice at NSA.

Another two weeks passed, and then I received word that our young patient was ready to come home. Sam, Sgt. Hung (an ARVN interpreter assigned to our battalion) and I went into Da Nang to pick her up. We found her sitting solemnly with a corpsman in the shade of the hospital triage building. I recognized the same tattered clothes she had been wearing at our first meeting at CAP 3-3. But what a difference!

"Would you believe that! Unreal!" exclaimed Sam. I had to agree. She had a remarkably good repair, much better than I had expected. Herb Burke, the plastic surgeon, had told me that her operation had gone well, but I wasn't quite prepared for the dramatic change where a thin red suture line and a minimal amount of soft tissue swelling were all that remained of her extensive defect.

Mai, however, did not seem impressed with her much-improved appearance, and as she obediently followed us into the jeep, there was no sign of recognition, only bewilderment and apprehension about what might happen next. No doubt, she had decided that her chances of seeing her parents and home again were not good. Were Viet Cong stories about giant Americans tormenting her fearful fantasies? The obligatory PX stop for some soda and candy brought no response. I looked at Sam and the sergeant, shaking my head as it was pretty clear we weren't making any headway in our efforts to reassure her. What else could we do to cheer her up? How about some new clothes, I thought. Would that do it? Probably not, but after all we really couldn't bring our patient back from the big city without an addition to her no doubt very limited wardrobe.

"Sgt. Hung," I said, "Do you think we can find some place to buy her some clothes?" It sure wasn't going to be as simple as making a trip to the nearest Sears store. Sgt. Hung, who was from Chu Lai originally, wasn't that familiar with Da Nang either, but he told us that we could go into the city itself and look around. Most of Da Nang was supposed to be off limits to military personnel who weren't on official business, but that regulation had been stretched many times for less worthwhile causes than ours.

Da Nang, once a relatively quiet port city that the French called Tourane, was now, on the surface, an overflowing hodge-podge of refugees, military of all kinds, prostitutes, and black marketeers. There were areas though, away from the red dirt and dust of the ramshackle outskirts where, with a little imagination, you could see glimpses of better times. For example, there was the boulevard along the river with its graceful royal poinciana trees and enclaves of palm-shaded white stucco buildings where well-to-do Vietnamese still managed to maintain some semblance of their former life style.

But signs of both physical and cultural decay were in evidence as we drove into the crowded streets along with the conglomeration of motor scooters, pedicabs, ARVN military vehicles, and an occasional classic old black Mercedes looking like a prop from a gangland movie. First we found a couple of Chinese stores, but to no avail, as their merchandise was inappropriate for a country child. How would a pink ruffled dress look on a little girl carrying water from the hamlet well in Phuoc Nunh? Finally we came to a large open market with its sea of people with the usual conical hats, like mollusks, as Graham Greene had once written. As we wandered up and down between the stalls, I was well aware that we were drawing plenty of stares. And why not, as I smiled, thinking of the picture we presented to the other shoppers: two six-foot-plus Marines, one Vietnamese man dressed like a Marine, and a tiny bare-footed Vietnamese girl wearing a ragged shirt and black pajama bottoms.

The stares turned to smiles however when Sgt. Hung explained the situation. Soon, Mai's wardrobe was increased by two sets of colorful pajamas, a large shade hat sporting a pink flower with a ribbon to tie under her chin, and for the finishing touch, a pair of bright green sandals. A knot of interested onlookers had gathered around us as Mai returned to make her debut following a quick change behind one of the stalls with the help of the woman who sold us the clothes. Now the transformation was nearly complete, except for one thing. Where was that elusive smile? Sam took a picture of the three of us—Mai peeking out from under her new hat and holding tightly onto a paper bundle containing her old clothes.

We drove past the sprawling Da Nang airfield as Phantoms and C-130s roared overhead. Mai sat in the back, expressionless, clutching a barely-touched can of orangeade. We turned south onto the Dai Loc road, leaving the cluttered shacks and ammunition dumps behind. Soon we were out in the country again. We passed the 7th Engineers "Freeway" sign, a nearly exact replica of a typical stateside interstate sign (except for numerous bullet holes) that read: Dai Loc Expressway, Speed Limit Day 35 MPH, Night Unlimited! Our small passenger still remained silent despite Sgt. Hung's efforts to convince her that she would soon be home.

When the familiar landmarks near CAP 3-3 began to appear, for the first time Mai started to perk up and take an interest in her surroundings. In a few more minutes we had arrived, and the enthusiastic reception that greeted us was just a preview of more to come. Mai sat quietly holding on to her bundle of clothes while the PFs, Marines, and giggling children crowded around, remarking about the miraculous change. Quickly, a patrol was sent off to Phuoc Ninh, and about fifteen minutes later, one of the children pointed out some figures approaching single file along the trail between the rice paddies. Mai watched closely, and as the group came nearer, she tried to do something that we had certainly never seen before. It was just a suggestion at first, but there it was—a funny little half smile.

Her father rushed up beaming and laughing excitedly. He took a close critical look and exclaimed something in rapid-fire Vietnamese. Then, smiling broadly, he proceeded to go around and vigorously shake hands, not once but twice, with all the Americans as well as the PFs who were watching this happy and heartwarming reunion. Later when some of the initial excitement had subsided, I took several snapshots of Mai, coaxing her to continue experimenting with that hesitant smile. What a contrast to the picture I had reluctantly taken of that sad and mournful girl of a month ago.

Morris turned to me saying, "You know sir, if we don't accomplish anything else here before I go back to the World, being around for this will help make it all seem worthwhile." Nodding in agreement, I thought to myself that all of a sudden I really understood how some physicians could leave the comforts and conveniences of our society behind to find fulfillment in practicing medicine in an area where no medical care was available. I'd sure never pictured myself in such a role, but now I realized what that was all about. Using the healing abilities we had acquired to help those people most in need, we could really make a difference, and their gratitude alone was sufficient reward.

Two weeks later, Sam and I were on our way to visit the local Vietnamese district chief when we had to slow down to pass a group of children returning from school, each one carrying notebooks and the customary little container of ink. One of them, a small girl wearing a hat with a large pink flower, spotted us and rushed up to the jeep. I looked down to see an inquisitive face with a shy smile. It was Mai. *"Chao Bac-si,"* (Hello Doctor) she said merrily, and with a peal of laughter trailing behind her, she rushed off to join her friends. I smiled but my eyes stung a little too as I watched her go.

Seventeen days before he was due to rotate back home, HM3 William Morris was killed when a jeep in which he was riding struck a mine. It was that kind of war.

Dai Loc children.

Mai (before). Near Phuoc Ninh hamlet.

Mai (after).

Mai. Shopping trip to Da Nang.

Dai Loc barber shop.

For peaceful happy
NEW YEAR'S

Tet, the first days of lunar year, has been, with the Vietnamese the days of joy and domestic affection, the occasion when families assemble to meditate over the ancestors.

The 7-day truce in fighting on Dinh-mui Tet which falls on Feb. 8, 1967 designed by the Presidium of the South Vietnam National Front for Liberation Central Committee will provide the soldiers and officials in the Saigon puppet army and government with the opportunies to enjoy a merry happy lunar New Year with their families at home and join in the spiritual worship of their forefathers.

The U.S. and satellite troops in South Vietnam also will have the happiness of enjoying the Front's humanitary policy to partake of the joyfulness of the traditional lunar New Year's.

Every criminal act in opposition with the sacred customs and laws trampling on the most venerable affection and the most solemn interest of the Vietnamese people will be strongly condemned by the whole people, even including your reluctant allies— the soldiers and officials in the puppet army and government. And all the military actions against the people and their Armed Forces during truce period or any enemy attempt violating the cease-fire order will be severely punished by the People's Armed Forces.

U.S. officers and men!

You must honor the Tet truce ordered by the S.V. N. F.L. and DEMAND THAT YOUR COMMANDING OFFICERS AND FELLOW SOLDIERS STRICTLY FOLLOW THE ARTICLES OF THE TET CEASE - FIRE ORDER OF THE S.V.L.A.F. COMMANDER-IN-CHIEF.

To have lasting peace and happy New Year's for Vietnamese as well as for American,

DEMAND THAT PEACE MUST BE RESTORED ON SOUTH VIETNAM, ALL U.S. TROOPS REPATRIATED.

THE QUANGDA PROVINCE

NATIONAL FRONT FOR LIBERATION

VC leaflet during Tet.

CHAPTER THREE

Dai Loc
Days

The dull shimmering haze of mid-afternoon's heat was fading into the relative cool of early evening. I was sitting in my hootch listening to Sam describe the exotic attractions of R & R in Bangkok when I heard Chief Carty's voice at the door.

"Doctor C," he said, "I just got a call from Major Cartwright down in the ville. They want you over at the dispensary. Something about some woman having trouble delivering twins."

"Chief, you've got to be kidding," I groaned. "OB isn't exactly my specialty, you know."

As I left, Sam helpfully reminded me to stop by the colonel's hootch to borrow some of his cigars to pass out.

I headed down the trail from our location in an old French Army campground on the hill above Dai Loc village. I tried to recall everything I could remember about the delivery of twins and didn't come up with much. I certainly had no practical experience except as a wide-eyed observer in medical school. Hoping that somehow the situation had corrected itself, I walked past the battered Quang Nam Province/USAID jeep ambulance into the courtyard. The dispensary consisted of an open-fronted roofed structure that doubled and tripled as a treatment triage area, storeroom, and records office. Set at right angles to this section was a small one-room building that served as a ward. Judging from the group of Vietnamese at the entrance, I knew it was time to put on my most confident manner and go inside to assess the situation. Be calm everybody, I thought, because the *bac-si* sure isn't.

Candlelight in the darkened interior revealed my patient lying on a mat with a small motionless form nearby, covered with a blood-stained mat. The woman was moaning softly as I tried to find out what had happened from *Bac-si* Manh, the district medical officer. Although he was titled *bac-si*, or doctor as I was, his training was limited to one year at the medical school in Hue plus a lot of practical experience. Working here with him were two midwives, one part-time nurse, and an ambulance driver. They provided all the medical care for the entire district as there were no Vietnamese physicians any closer than Da Nang.

Bac-si Manh told me that the midwife delivered the first baby about an hour ago. The infant struggled feebly to breathe for a few minutes and then died. However, he said that there was still one more baby that wouldn't come out. I kneeled down in the dim light and examined her. She was bleeding a little, and I could feel an arm hanging down into the birth canal. I flashed back to a picture in our obstetrics textbook of a situation where the baby lies transversely and wedged down into the neck of the uterus with one arm hanging down into the vagina. All that my whirring brain could remember otherwise was that it was a high-risk problem, and the outcome often was not good even in the best of hands, and mine sure weren't the best. There were all kinds of terrible things that could happen, including rupture of the uterus. The infant was probably not going to survive no matter what, so the main concern was for the mother at this point.

Quickly I tried some abdominal manipulation recalling that sometimes the position could be changed by external methods. But nothing good happened, and the women began to moan loudly as her uterus contracted down, trying to expel its remaining contents. It was beginning to look really bad at this point, so I decided to tell *Bac-si* Manh to go over to Major Cartwright, the district chief's army advisor, and have him ask for a medevac chopper. At the provincial hospital in Hoi An there was a team of Navy physicians, including one obstetrician working with the meagre, overwhelmed Vietnamese staff. In the meantime, I decided to start an IV with dextrose and water so that if she began to hemorrhage, we could at least give her some fluid.

We carried her on a stretcher over to the makeshift helipad near the Major's office accompanied by lots of curious children and her anxious relatives and friends. The sky was beginning to darken now, and I knew that if no helicopter were available right away, there would be none until morning, because flights at night in this part of the country were great targets for Charlie. We waited on the porch of a nearby school building fronting the village square. The woman, who was probably in her late twenties, seemed a little more comfortable and was quieter now.

In about twenty-five minutes, I heard the sound of two approaching helicopters off to the west—and then something else. The woman groaned a little, and I looked down to see her face contorted in effort. Quickly I pulled back the green army blanket and checked her. The second baby was coming! Somehow with continued contractions, the baby had turned enough so that delivery feet first or breech was now possible. I presided over the birth of an unfortunately dead second twin. The placenta followed with surprisingly not much bleeding. She gave me a wan smile and fell back on the stretcher in exhaustion. Just then Capt. Cartwright's head appeared over the watching crowd, "These guys are really hot to get out of here. What the hell is going on anyway."

I gulped, "Would you believe she just had her other baby. It looks like she is going to be all right, so we won't need a medevac after all. Tell 'em thanks." I yelled after him.

I was glad that the Vietnamese pressing around us provided a place to hide and be spared some of the crew's comments about having to fly out for nothing and about these damn doctors who didn't know what they were doing.

As the helicopters roared angrily off, we all paraded back to the dispensary. The accompanying children were dashing around playing and laughing, and the mood of the whole group seemed friendly, with lots of smiles in my direction. Was I ever relieved that the crisis was past, and at least on the maternal side, there were probably not going to be any complications, although infection was still a concern. Still, it didn't seem like a time for a lot of happiness what with two dead infants.

A little puzzled, I turned towards *Bac-si* Manh with a questioning look. *"Dai-uy Bac-si,"* he told me with a smile, "the people believe that your medicine in the bottle made the baby come out and saved the woman's life. You are a hero."

The IV? I'd forgotten all about it—but there was nothing in it except sugar water. What a way to get a good reputation, I laughed to myself. Modern medicine's miracle drug—a little dextrose and water and a lot of luck saved the day. I just was hoping that there were no further obstetrical emergencies to test my new found cure-all. I was a hero in Dai Loc for the moment, but I was a dirty word in the helicopter squadron.

The Dai Loc dispensary was the focal point of our MEDCAP

activities during our several months in that area. MEDCAP, or medical civil action program, was felt to be a valuable adjunct to our overall war effort by some of the Marine Corps brass; others more or less gave lip service to the program. In addition to providing much needed and generally unavailable medical care, the idea of course was to win support for the Vietnamese government and allied forces with hope that more information and help would be forthcoming in areas frequented by the VC and NVA. Realistically, the average Vietnamese peasant, no matter how pro-government his sentiments, could not afford to be too openly sympathetic unless he was in an area where 24-hour protection was available. The RVN yellow flag with three red stripes might fly proudly during the day, but during the night most of the countryside still belonged to the Viet Cong.

Medically however, depending on the interests and time available to the Navy medical personnel with the Marines, it was possible to help many Vietnamese who might otherwise have access to no more sophisticated medical care than the local traditional Chinese apothecary shop, or if living in a larger village like Dai Loc, perhaps a dispensary facility. Vietnamese physicians were in extremely short supply. Besides skeleton staff in the large civilian hospitals, the majority were in the ARVN or provided private care to wealthy Vietnamese in the larger cities.

In the Dai Loc region, most Marine combat casualties could be medevaced directly to nearby Da Nang from the field instead of through the BAS for triage. As a result, besides spending time with the usual sick-call problems, mostly infectious diseases and assorted trauma, we had more opportunities for MEDCAP activities in this particular location than in most. Our other battalion surgeon, Harry Ashford, chose not to get involved in MEDCAP too much. He felt (and I had to agree with him at times) that it was just too disorganized and inefficient to accomplish anything. He was actually somewhat intrigued by combat operations and even tried to talk the colonel into letting him go out in the field. This practice didn't occur very often, the argument generally being that there wasn't much sense in risking a medical officer to do the same job as a corpsman. That was fine with me. I felt I could do a lot more for the Marines in one piece, so I adhered to the old military axiom of not volunteering for anything most of the time.

The scene at the Dai Loc dispensary, especially in the beginning, was typical of the majority of our MEDCAP trips. There were swarms of people—especially children—with often nearly as many spectators as patients. As a rule we would see quite a few who would manufacture vague complaints for the novelty of the occasion—*dau bung* (stomach

36

ache), tired all the time, or cough for six months were commonplace among the older adults. Maintaining order with the crush of people, the young, old, sick and curious, required almost strong-arm tactics at times. An overcrowded county hospital waiting room looked peaceful and orderly in comparison. A lot of the problems, it seemed, could have been prevented by just a little soap and water plus some decent plumbing.

Skin infections, especially boils, were very common. After draining eight to ten on one baby's head early in my MEDCAP career, I earned the distinguished title of *"Bac-si Pus"* from that day onward, thanks to one of our interpreters. We treated many children arbitrarily for intestinal parasites, and worm medicine went as fast as cold remedies in a pediatric clinic in the U.S.A. Diagnosis was usually based on physical examination and clinical instinct, as it was difficult to get any real history about the problem with an overworked interpreter. My own supply of Vietnamese especially in the first few months was limited to such basics as: "What's wrong?," "Where does it hurt?," and "Take two pills every six hours." It was good more for laughs than results. The routine was a throwback to the days of practicing medicine without the benefit of even the most routine and basic laboratory and x-ray studies.

Requests for vitamins were frequent, and there were some Dai Loc villagers who came in to the dispensary to get regular injections from *Bac-si* Manh's nurse. But at what a price! They had some old glass syringes and a tray with some very dull needles which were sterilized by pouring alcohol and firing the whole works with a match. Subsequently I would watch with a grimace as the nurse struggled to push in the nearly blunt needle. The popularity of vitamin shots increased rapidly when we were able to come up with some extra boxes of our own disposable needles. In fact, seeing the sharp, relatively painless needles, the village barber, who had an infectious skin rash, helped us decide on our treatment plan by gesturing emphatically toward his buttocks with a jabbing motion. "Be-nee-ceellin," he repeated over and over until we obliged him.

Figuring their duties rated special treatment, PFs would sometimes push their way through the crowd demanding an examination for "chest pain" or similar questionable complaints. They would smile and talk to their friends while being checked, as though our examination would not only increase their status but would also provide magical protection against the VC. Unfortunately, we would invariably see civilians who were the inevitable victims: A middle-aged woman with a GSW (gunshot wound) of the left hip with probable fracture; a ten-year-old boy with a one-day-old very bad GSW of the right elbow with an exposed, shattered bone protruding through torn muscle plus multiple fragment wounds in his leg; an older boy with a partially destroyed hand looking dazedly on as Manh applied lots of Merthiolate (common) and a dressing. Some ARVN soldiers brought in a patient with a foot wound who was allegedly an NVA corpsman. He was very young and very stoic, no doubt expecting the worst, and he had a bag which contained medicine from China as well as a lot from England and France.

The worst casualties were medevaced through the army advisor to one of the hopelessly overcrowded civilian hospitals where most of the time there was much delay and little chance for a reasonable outcome. Poor unfortunate people. How they suffered. Many times it was hard to get any real feel for what actually happened. Sometimes we would only get the answer that they came from an area with "beaucoup VC" or that they were out in a freefire zone where they had been told not to go. How many others were there who never even made it as far as the dispensary?

After becoming a more familiar face, I even got an invitation from one of the local merchants to make a house call in the village to see his daughter, who had been very sick recently with a strange fever. Sgt. Hung and I went to check on her after our regular battalion afternoon sick-call. We found her lying on a low bamboo bed in a darkened room behind their store. She was about 18 and apparently for the past two and a half weeks or so, had been running fevers off and on with periods of delirium. *Bac-si* Manh had seen her earlier and prescribed a whole collection of medicines that had been picked up at a pharmacy in Da Nang. And what a list it was—there were at least five different kinds including some penicillin, a type of French broad-spectrum antibiotic which included vitamin B12 plus some other vitamins and cold medicine. Examining her, I found that, besides a fever of 102 F and generalized weakness, there were no definite abnormalities. Upon further questioning, I discovered that she had had some red spots last week that went away.

Even among our well-immunized Marines, FUO (fever of unknown origin) was a common initial diagnosis. Usually it turned out to be some type of viral infection followed by occasional cases of malaria, dengue fever or an uncommon problem like the tongue twister, tsutsugamushi disease (scrub typhus). This girl, however, had something different. In fact I thought, it seemed a little like—I checked her pulse, which was rather slow in spite of her fever—typhoid! It had to be! Manh had been treating her with everything in the book except the one antibiotic that probably would be the best bet. I would have to diplomatically suggest to him that we try some chloramphenicol that I could get from our own supplies.

One year ago I would have been raked over the coals for using such a drug with its potentially life-threatening side effects without the benefit of appropriate laboratory studies. But it seemed like a reasonable move in this setting where even the usual isolation techniques and careful hygienic measures had to be practically ignored, and especially since she had refused to be taken to the hospital in Da Nang or Hoi An. I gave them some Tylenol for her fever plus some medication for nausea and tried to smile encouragingly, not letting them know that things were not exactly up to par by our standards.

As in most Vietnamese house calls, there were a few others in need of medical attention. In particular there was a relative who had been "sick in the same way." We walked out in back down a path next to a flooded rice paddy to a cluster of houses. Scattering some chickens on the way, we went into a small hardpacked courtyard with a two tiered-pigeon roost in one corner. The house itself had a sturdy bamboo framework with plaited woven mat material for walls and a tightly thatched roof. Lying on a mat in the cool, dim interior was a young man who looked like a Nazi concentration camp victim. Sunken dull eyes looked out at us from a body that was virtually a skeleton. He had some dried purplish-red material on his chest and arms which Hung said was Chinese medicine. Supposedly he had been ill with fever and diarrhea for three to four weeks and had not been able to eat for quite a while, needless to say! Could it be a burned out case of typhoid? Hung said that he also would not leave Dai Loc and go to the hospital. I decided that maybe we could return with the jeep and get him over to the dispensary for some IV fluids for a few days at least.

On the way back we stopped at the first home for one more patient, a five-year-old girl who had a three-week-old badly infected, abscessed dog bite on her thigh. She was not at all excited about being taken by the giant *bac-si* to the BAS for treatment. Nevertheless, we brought our small patient, now protesting loudly, back up the hill with her father where, with some reinforcements, I was able to incise the wound and put in a drain. Back down she went, still very unhappy despite a Woody Woodpecker puppet, and I could only hope that maybe tomorrow when I checked on her she would have forgiven me a little. Then finally it was back to the dispensary for our cadaverous gentleman, who looked even worse in better light. Hopefully, if I could keep him out of the hands of his favorite Chinese medicine man, he could get a start back toward regaining his strength. Later that night in the BAS, I found a reference in our textbook of internal medicine to typhoid patients in the pre antibiotic era who became very debilitated because of lack of adequate nursing and nutritional supportive care. We weren't quite that far back in medical time here, but occasionally it was close.

One morning a few weeks later I was down at Major Cartwright's watching his pet monkey steal pens out of my pocket. Just then I looked up to see one of Hotel Company's jeeps come speeding up and slam to a jolting, dusty stop in front of the door. In the back seat were two Vietnamese women supporting a young girl who was slumped between them.

The driver jumped out and said hurriedly, "Sir, they carried her up to the CP a little while ago. She's hurt really bad. I'm not sure exactly what happened, but the corpsman just told me to bring her over here fast."

I had a sinking feeling as I listened because I noticed that the girl had a battle dressing around her head. We got her outside and up on the floor of the porch. She was around 12 or 13 years old, pale, and unconscious, and upon removing the bloody bandage, my heart sank even further. There was a small, neat entrance wound high on her forehead, but in the back was a large, ragged exit wound filled with thick, dark-jelly clots of blood. Instinctively I yelled at the Major to check and see if there was any chance for a fast medevac to Da Nang where there was a neurosurgeon, but I knew she had practically no chance. However, the wound seemed quite high, and I thought that maybe somehow we could stabilize her with some saline and plasma. Her pulse was very weak, and she was so shocky I knew it would be hard to find a vein for an IV. I worked desperately with her mother sobbing and moaning behind me. But the girl was slipping fast, and a few minutes later she took a couple of gasping breaths and then was gone. Stunned by the tragedy that had shattered the morning sunshine, I stood aside as her mother threw herself over the still form. Questions raced through my head as I watched the anguish before me. How did it happen? Were we responsible somehow? Could she have been saved if she could have been treated right away?

I helped carry her body back to the dispensary in an awful funeral procession accompanied by the wailing mother, the other woman from the jeep, and some curious onlookers. Knowing that I needed to go out to Hotel Company's position anyway, I tried to make them understand that we could go back in a jeep, but when PFC Armstrong, the BAS driver, and I returned, they were gone. As we drove slowly through Dai Loc, up ahead near the bridge there were two women with a bamboo stretcher suspended from a carrying pole. On it was someone wrapped in a mat, blood-stained at one end. There was no need to wonder who the victim was. We stopped the jeep and loaded them all in and headed west along the road toward Hill 63.

The mother was calm now with only a glazed look—no tears,

completely in control. Her courage seemed to symbolize the strength of the Vietnamese people, who had to adjust to a nearly endless wartime existence where there were often such burdens to bear. Later I was to find out just how brave she really was. She had known only that she must somehow take her daughter's body home, and she had set out to do it the best way she knew—by walking and carrying her daughter on an improvised stretcher back to their hamlet—a 20-minute jeep ride at least.

How these people endured! How they worked and toiled in the paddies with the most primitive of tools. Violent death, like monsoon rains, mud, dust, and illness, were just some of the components in the life of the Vietnamese peasant that had to be accepted. We passed some people threshing rice in a huge basket set up in the field. Everything looked so damn deceptively peaceful now. Shortly we stopped to let our passengers off about a half mile before Hotel Company's Hill 63. I doubt I'll ever forget the picture of the two women walking quickly away on the trail between the paddies, their grim burden swaying gently between them.

Soon I was walking into the bunker that served as a makeshift aid station to find Lyman, Hotel Company's senior corpsman. He looked up and said slowly, "Doc, I know she didn't make it, did she?" I shook my head. "I tried to get her a medevac but the CO said there wouldn't be anything until afternoon. Couldn't even get a damn needle in to give her some plasma."

"I couldn't either," I replied. "I really don't think we could have helped her no matter what. Did you find out anything about what happened?"

"Yeah, I did, but I wish I hadn't," he answered, grimacing. "It was a VC assassination squad. Her father was a school teacher, and I guess he made the hit list. The sons of bitches came in early this morning and dragged him out. They tied him to the corner of his house, shot him in the arms and legs and then cut him open." Disembowelment, I thought—the horror of it was unbelievable. Lyman continued, "Then they threw grenades down the bunker where the rest of the family was hiding. The girl tried to run off, and she got zapped. The mother wasn't there so she's the only one left."

I felt a rising tide of rage as he was talking and for an insane moment, I wanted to run outside, grab an M16 and blow away the first VC suspect I could find. In the distance I heard Lyman go on.

"It's been a bad day, sir. We went out on patrol yesterday, and there was this prisoner I worked on for awhile so he could be brought in for

41

questioning. This morning a Marine from first platoon came up to me and asked for some alcohol to preserve this ear he had. Turned out to belong to the same guy who supposedly was shot trying to escape. I just can't believe this place anymore, I really can't."

I stared at the sandbagged wall without seeing. "Hey, the VC don't have a patent on inhumanity, Lyman," I said slowly, shaking my head.

The pain and sadness of that day was submerged in work on our latest BAS project, the famous MEDCAP wagon. Usually on MEDCAP trips we hauled our medical gear in two large boxes that inevitably ended up in a hopeless disarray of bottles of pills and disinfectant, bars of soap, dressing material, and assorted instruments. Chief Carty came up with the idea to build compartments onto a small jeep trailer with the final result being an old-style, wild west travelling medical-show wagon. All hands pitched in, and we soon had a unique one-of-a-kind, portable dispensary that turned out to be an attraction in its own right in addition to providing us with a very unaccustomed organization of our medical supplies. The plywood sides could be swung up to reveal Vietnamese health posters for some on-the-spot patient education. We even had various medicine instruction signs that could be used in a pinch when there were no interpreters around. The project was a great success; we even rated an article plus pictures in the *Stars and Stripes* as well as an official blessing from the commanding general of the 3rd Marine Division, who was passing through with the usual trailing procession of starched colonels and aides.

One of the first appearances of the wagon in public was at a "County Fair" held near Hoa Luong, a hamlet with many apparent VC connections. County fairs were joint USMC-Vietnamese military and civic action programs designed to re-establish government control over the people. Basically, a village or hamlet was surrounded by a cordon force of Marines. Then a Vietnamese unit went through the area and brought all civilians in the enclosed area to a central collecting point, bringing their identity documents, cooking utensils, and valuables with them. They were checked through to a nearby designated area where they were to be bombarded with government propaganda and receive medical care as well as donated clothing and food. In the meantime, back in the village area, the search force was conducting a systematic and thorough inspection of the area for tunnels and VC concealed weapons. Success in these operations was somewhat debatable. On paper it all looked effective, but in reality there were many opportunities for slip-ups.

However, our MEDCAP wagon was a big hit. We set up in one corner of the enclosure, and soon found a couple of local kids for interpreters and odd job duties. In a short time, the word was out, and we had a steady supply of customers with ailments ranging from nonexistent to those requiring the services of *Bac-si* Pus.

While we were going strong, the healthy citizens were being barraged with speakers and propaganda about the advantage of siding with the government, which no doubt fell on quite a few deaf ears, as many VC friends and relatives were probably in the crowd. Later, cooking fires were started, and a conglomeration of blackened cooking utensils materialized. Tents were spilling occupants, sleeping mats, various family belongings, and new toys out the sides. Children were everywhere under foot, and some volleyball games were underway. It really began to seem like a big summer picnic as nightfall came.

Sam and I were passing time around a dying tea fire as he tried out a personalized version of the people-to-people program—in this case USMC to *co* (unmarried girl). Suddenly we were abruptly brought back to reality as a staccato burst of automatic weapon fire sent everyone diving for cover. I decided that the best place for me was as flat on the ground as possible right where I was. I tried to become part of the red dirt itself, but couldn't seem to get anywhere low enough. Another burst whistled overhead of what was referred to as "small arms fire." I always was struck by the inappropriateness of that phrase, as there was there was nothing small about its potential for destructive effects on one's person.

Is this the way it starts, I thought as I sneaked a look out through the perimeter into the misty paddies, which looked like spooky Scottish moors in the full moonlight. Knowing there was a platoon of Marines out there as a blocking force was reassuring, but all of a sudden I couldn't help feeling very vulnerable. Without much difficulty, I began to envision VC slipping into position in the shadows of the paddy edges and waiting for the moment to charge. However, after the rattle of some distant fire and a pop of a flare, the warm, humid night settled over us again like a welcome cover.

Nobody was hit, and it apparently was only some high sniper fire from a distant tree line, but the whole episode didn't make for a very restful night. We treated a few minor lacerations and sprains that occurred in the first rush for some cover and then spent another few hours playing around with 14 or 15 kids who decided they were going to spend the night at our tent. There were free massages (five children to one corpsman) and all-out free-for-alls until well past midnight. The remainder of the night was spent trying to avoid thoughts of Custer's

Last Stand, but fortunately Victor Charles decided to leave us alone. Finally, the mysterious, ominous shapes of night turned into familiar and welcome surroundings with the coming of dawn. Our medicine show had survived to hit the road again.

In another few weeks we began to hear rumblings about the battalion moving out and heading north. Rumor turned into the official word, and our Dai Loc days were soon to come to an end. The last few days were busy ones, but still pervaded with a certain sadness, knowing that I was leaving a lot of friends here. The last night before we were due to be heli-lifted out to Da Nang for points north, I went over to see the gang of kids by the wire. We joked about what it was going to be like coming back some day. Ly was going to be a beautiful *co*. Johnny scoffed at that comment and said she would be fat with "plenty baby san." It was not proving to be very easy to say good-bye to my young friends, whose smiling faces and laughter had brightened many evenings. Finally, getting ready to leave, I reached over the barbed wire to shake Johnny's hand. As I did he gave me a card in return, which turned out to be a very Western-style sentimental Easter card which read, "Happy Easter to my Sweetheart" over a large purple tulip. On the inside he had written:

Souvenir
My name Johnny
Souvenir dotor a picture
My boy — *Dai-uy* # one
—CALBWILL—USMC
I love you every day # one
You same thing my brother
My name Johnny and CALBWELL frean # one

Coming from the ten-year-old boisterous, junior Marine ringleader of the gang, the card was a real surprise. My heart really went out to Johnny and the rest of these kids whose futures were so uncertain. I solemnly thanked him, and waving once more, I walked reluctantly and sadly up the hill toward what was left of our tent.

Later, after one more trip to pick up some gear from the Dai Loc dispensary, I was walking slowly up the familiar path in the soft darkness of early evening when I heard a voice coming from a figure standing by one of the huts. The flickering light of a kerosene lamp dimly illuminated the face of the dispensary jeep ambulance driver. He was a slight man with a wisp of a Ho Chi Minh beard.

"Bac-si di dau?" He peered questioningly at me. (Where are you going, doctor?)

I strung together a few words of my best Vietnamese and answered, *"Chung ta di di Phu Bai ngay mai."* (Tomorrow we go to Phu Bai.)

He grabbed my hand and continued to shake it even as I started to go. It was a warm and unexpected gesture. I thought of my dinnertime discussion with John Masterson, a Hotel battery lieutenant with no appreciation for anything Vietnamese. He had been telling me that he couldn't understand why I wasted my time hanging around "those worthless gooks." Yes, John, I thought as I stumbled up the rest of the narrow trail, why should I bother with these people when all I get is a handshake and a heartfelt thank you?

It was a melancholy *bac-si* that finally dropped off to sleep that night. The flares popped and drifted down like twisting yellow snakes in the warm dark sky. Distant artillery fire echoed dully in the night, and the war continued—but for me Dai Loc would soon be just another set of bittersweet memories.

Assistant Bac-si. Dai Loc dispensary.

Dai Loc girl and rice paddies.

Family and house with anti-VC banner. Dai Loc village.

One size fits all. Refugee village near Dai Loc.

Bus, before.

Local bus, after VC mine.

Dai Loc bridge and children.

Traveling Medical Show - Vietnamese style.

Free ride time. Main Street, Dai Loc.

Phong Dien village dispensary.
Volunteer ambulance attendants.

CHAPTER FOUR

Father Matthieu

I was drifting down the placid River of Perfumes near Hue, the old capital of Vietnam. I was a mandarin in a gilded sampan that was guided by a crew of stunning women. They were dressed in shimmering, electric blue *ao dai*, the traditional costume of gossamer tunic split to the waist worn over white silk pants. The peaceful scene was suddenly broken by a shout from one of the crew, and there was a crunch. The eager river poured in, and I was awash in cold water that brought me back to sodden reality. Rolled in a leaky poncho, I blinked awake to find the dark skies now opening up with a monsoon-calibre deluge. There were no real raindrops; it seemed to be just coming down in huge streams. The time had come to beat a fast retreat to the regimental aid station.

After fumbling around for several minutes in a saturated pile of gear trying to find a flashlight, I stumbled off with two of the corpsmen past the ghostly profile of some 155mm howitzers. Splashing and sliding around in the mud, I thought of our recently vacated Dai Loc camp which right now seemed like a prime R & R destination. We were located now in some low, rolling dusty hills west of Highway 1, about halfway between Hue and Quang Tri. Arriving earlier that day in the late afternoon after an interminable bone-jarring convoy ride from Phu Bai, we had found our designated location to be definitely the most unimproved area in what amounted to a fairly large combat base. Since most of the battalion hadn't arrived yet, we would be living in style like grunts in the field for a few days at least. There were two other battalions here in addition to the 4th Marine Regimental Headquarters, plus several supporting units. Our overall objective was to cut off access from Co Bi

Thanh Tan, a valley in the mountains to the west, which was reported to harbor several large mainforce NVA units. To the east was the infamous Street Without Joy—a hard-core Communist area dating back to Viet Minh days. In an ironic turn of events, Bernard Fall, the author who had originally given the region its notoriety, had recently been killed there during a patrol when he was somehow compelled to return for another visit.

After wandering all over the place, we eventually made it to the RAS, which wasn't exactly dry either. I ended up sleeping on a stretcher that was the operating table for their minor-surgery area. I was finally getting to sleep when a Marine was brought in who had been bitten by several centipedes. No doubt they were trying to get out of the rain as well.

The next morning it was dry-out time, at least for a brief hour when the sun relented and made a short appearance. What a mess! At first glance it looked like it had rained for weeks, but just a short downpour, Vietnam-style, was all that was required for the resulting quagmire. It looked like monsoon season all over again, with thick red mud in abundant supply. I sat on a couple of old ammo boxes outside the minor surgery tent watching one of the corpsmen open the back of his camera and curse the elements out loud as mud and water poured out. What was there worth taking a picture of around here anyway, I muttered as I found my own camera suffering from the same ailment.

After that soggy morning's inauspicious beginning, life at Co Bi Thanh Tan started to improve, so that in another week and a half we had carved out a fairly respectable battalion area out of our piece of the raw, red hillside. The time did not pass without quite a few noteworthy incidents. For example, there was the great mustache crackdown. We had a daily battalion briefing where the medical officer would routinely contribute fascinating items such as the latest figure in the number of cases of gastroenteritis.

One afternoon from out of a clear blue sky, the colonel announced that it had come to his attention that facial hair was getting a little abundant. He continued saying that he didn't "care to see my men looking sloppy and it also happened that I'm in a position to do something about it, so as of 0800 tomorrow morning, there will be no more mustaches in the battalion."

A black, mustachioed NCO next to me rolled his eyes upwards as though the colonel had just ordered him to cut off a finger or two. Reactions were similar elsewhere, but most of the Marines were accustomed to such strange commands. After all, this was the outfit in which shaving gear was carried into combat, and when the colonel shaved, the word was passed for everybody to do likewise. A top-notch elite fighting unit must look sharp at all times even when out in the weeds, was the thinking. Such attention to appearance was lost on some Marines, and the old familiar expression "The apple is sweet but the Corps sucks" was heard in some quarters again.

Also there was the Kaopectate Kaper. Outbreaks of gastroenteritis or "Uncle Ho's revenge" were very commonplace, especially when the battalion was out in the field. A little untreated paddy water was almost a guarantee of some intestinal difficulties, but back in camp, contaminated water wasn't supposed to be a problem. However, about a week after we arrived, somebody decided to support the local economy and buy some ice to treat the mess hall's Kool Aid. Twenty-four hours later, the battalion's 4-holers were overrun with eager customers with lines forming even at 2:00 or 3:00 a.m. Fortunately, most of the battalion was out in the field, but for those lucky troops remaining behind, the uniform of the day included a four-ounce bottle of kaopectate and paregoric, plus a steady diet of Lomotil diarrhea pills. Even the unthinkable happened—the colonel's personal 1-holer was used by someone else (under the cover of darkness of course). In such an emergency, however, that kind of a capital offense surely would have been overlooked. Fortunately, the secret started and stopped safely with me.

MEDCAP activity here was limited to occasional trips to the local dispensary on the outskirts of Phong Dien, a village similar in size to Dai Loc, and to the refugee villages located nearby just east of Highway 1. One of the refugee areas was Buddhist and one Catholic, and we were very careful to give them both equal time from the standpoint of number of visits as well as donated supplies. Of the two, the Catholic village was the most notable, primarily because of the efforts of a remarkable 39-year-old priest named Father Matthieu. Educated in France, his family name was Nguyen Van Nghi, and prior to coming to Phong Dien he had served as chaplain for the ARVN training camp at Nha Trang.

Over the period of the past three years, he had turned a refugee area consisting of a cluster of weather-beaten shacks out in the sand flat into a model village unlike anything I had ever seen in Vietnam. The houses, each with a neat fence and gateway, were laid out in blocks lined with newly planted cypress and eucalyptus trees bordering well-defined sandy roads. He had built his church adjacent to a centrally located plaza, which was flanked by the school building and several small shops. Materials had been obtained mainly through overcoming the endless mass of Vietnamese governmental bureaucracy, and the construction itself was a great tribute to Father Matthieu's ability to organize and inspire his village. Subsequently he had been able to make the village nearly self-supporting by initiating a whole variety of simple trades ranging from clothes and woven hats for the Phong Dien market to a bicycle-repair shop which he had just recently opened. At the same time his ability to elicit contributions from various relief organizations as well as supplies from nearby military units was legendary.

It was clear from my first MEDCAP visit to Father Matthieu's village that things were definitely a little different. Instead of the usual chaos of milling prospective patients and onlookers, we had the most orderly sick call imaginable. Father Matthieu did the interpreting, and we saw our patients in his small dispensary that had a meagre assortment of donated French and American medical supplies. Not only did relative peace and quiet prevail, but each person, even the children, who were very clean, thanked me with a little bow.

Later over some tea and slices of watermelon, Father Matthieu talked about his plans for the village. He was tall for a Vietnamese and was quite sturdy-appearing in his black cassock. Speaking English very well, he was mentioning his educational goals for the children.

"The future of my country depends on our children's education," he said, "and in spite of the war and the Communists, somehow we have to keep the schools functioning."

He had already opened a secondary school and had plans for a high school eventually. I asked him about the Viet Cong. Fingering the simple wooden cross he wore around his neck, he smiled and told me that he didn't think they would harm him, because he had never done any harm to them.

In the following weeks I saw a lot of Father Matthieu during the course of our visits. As I got to know him better, it was easy to see why he was so well respected and loved by his villagers, and also why he was so effective in getting what he needed for his various projects. He was quite aggressive and pushed up to a certain point. Then, knowing just when to back off, it was almost impossible to turn him down because his cause was so just. His brand of pragmatism, piety, and sincerity served him very well, and with the arrival of the Americans, we also were approached at every opportunity to do our share. Tin, concrete, and various building materials had found their way to his village courtesy of the Marines, and we were able to take care of most of their medical needs. I even patronized his village barber shop, and for my 120 piastres, in addition to a haircut, I received a shampoo, massage, and vigorous neck-cracking from an elderly Vietnamese who addressed me as *"Mon Capitaine."*

Up on our hill, life with the grunts had settled into the routine of the tedious, the unexpected, and the tragi-comic. Our battalion had been participating in a much ballyhooed multi-unit operation in the mountains to the west. However, after nearly three weeks, the result had been little contact and much frustration. Medevac flights had brought in many non-combat type problems such as jungle rot (various skin infections), gastrointestinal difficulties, and heat casualties. Fox company had just come in from the field for a few days of relative luxurious living.

That particular night we were sitting around the battalion aid station, now a well-sandbagged split-level masterpiece, listening to accounts of a recent Hong Kong R & R returnee while the usual card game was underway. A big movie screen had been set up next to the mess tent, and a Western shoot'em up was being featured. Suddenly a chilling burst of rifle fire jolted us out of our comfort zone, especially since it appeared to be very definitely inside the perimeter.

"Oh-h-h, Sh—," said Chief Carty as we all grabbed flak jackets and helmets, trying to maintain some semblance of cool, nonchalant veterans, accustomed to such interruptions. Heading outside toward our bunkers, we noticed an approaching group of Marines who seemed to be restraining one struggling figure as relative quiet once again prevailed.

As they reached us, one of the Marines said, "Excuse us, sir, but we've got one very drunk Marine here, and the lieutenant says for you to make it official."

He was a tall, gangly, nearly 100% Sioux PFC by the name of Paul Whitedeer. He had been doing some serious drinking with his buddies while watching the movie where his people were being mowed down by the palefaces. Letting out some wild unintelligible yells, he suddenly grabbed his M16, jumped up and began to subject the movie screen to some intense small arms fire. For these untimely outbursts, PFC Whitedeer was headed for the stockade in Da Nang, and I was supposed to document his condition. The diagnosis was easily established, and the mumbling, incoherent, and very strong Whitedeer was taken away. Later his platoon commander told me that the Sioux was a holy terror in the field when sober, but tended to have alcohol problems in camp, needless to say.

Shaking my head in amazement, I returned to the BAS to get the word that I was supposed to show up at 0730 at LZ Scat to join the rest of the battalion in the field. Harry had come in with Fox company and was not

59

feeling well, so *Bac-si* Caldwell was the man of the hour. Spending a restless night, I awoke once early in the morning to the sound of some distant explosions and the usual sound of sporadic small arms fire.

The LZ was an oven by 10 o'clock. With all my gear, I was definitely overdressed for sunbathing, and my ride to the battalion wilderness retreat had failed to materialize. It seemed that there was a direct connection between mouth and sweat glands, as my two canteens were emptying very fast. Several choppers had come and gone, but nobody knew anything about a resupply run to 2/4. Finally after another hour of futility, one of our jeep ambulances came rattling up.

"Would you believe it's all off? The latest is that they're all coming in tomorrow," said the corpsman shaking his head in agreement to my comments about the Corps.

Back at the BAS at around high noon, I threw my pack down and slumped against the sandbagged wall in disgust. The chief came outside, sat down next to me, and listened for awhile to the highlights of my morning.

Then he said softly, "Doctor C, it's been a bad day all around so far. We just got a call from A-Med. It was about Father Matthieu." The tone of his voice told me what to expect. It couldn't be anything but bad news, and it was.

The chief continued, "Early this morning a VC squad came into his village and went to his house. He refused to come out so they stood back and blasted the place with B-40 rockets from all sides. Some ARVN from the subsector advisor's unit drove them off after a brief firefight. Somehow he survived, but he was in real bad shape with frag wounds in the abdomen and the liver. He died in the OR, doc—he didn't have a chance."

I sat stunned and sickened for a long time, wondering how it could be possible that such a tragedy could be allowed to occur to such a remarkable individual. Rage welled up inside of me as I thought of Viet Cong flag wavers back home. Come over here and see your heroes in action, I thought bitterly. But for Father Matthieu, who believed he had nothing to fear from the Viet Cong, there was nothing left but his legacy of unforgettable devotion and dedication to his people, and the inspiration he gave to all of those who knew him.

Somewhere in the distance I heard a voice call to me, "Hey Doctor C, you got your orders back to Phu Bai."

Father Matthieu (center).
Phong Dien Catholic refugee village.

Phong Dien Villagers. MEDCAP.

Hand-to-hand combat.

Irrigation project near Hue.

CHAPTER FIVE

City Of The Emperors

Phu Bai wasn't actually a distinct large village, but a conglomeration of small villages and hamlets 14 kilometers south of Hue. The Hue- Phu Bai airport was located in this area just east of Highway 1, and A-Med itself had grown up across the road from the battered terminal. Walking into the hospital compound was familiar ground for me as it was here over ten months ago that I had started my career as a Vietnam GMO. A large triage area fronted the road with adjoining operating rooms, minor surgery, and wards extending to the rear. There a large sand courtyard was surrounded by the standard collection of hardbacks, now more weathered and worn by over three-quarters of a year of blistering sun, blowing sand, and monsoon rain. Since A-Med was technically supposed to be a secure area, the rear of the compound was protected by a volleyball court, some storage facilities, and directly in back of the hootch that I was going to call home, an exclusive 1-hole franchise of the Medical Library. Overall, the place hadn't really changed much since my earlier stint except that now there were more GMOs around, some of whom, as in my case, had rotated back to the medical battalion from infantry assignments.

I sat around the hootch catching up with the latest rumors and swapping war stories with Don Martin, an internist from Seattle. He and I had first run into each other at Camp Pendleton and started out together here at A-Med last summer. He was an easy-going, studious individual who rolled with the punches of Vietnam quite well. After spending nine months in the Da Nang area, Don had returned to Phu Bai about four weeks ago and was now running MEDCAP. Both of us were now close to being genuine short-timers with only a couple of months to go. The nervous, apprehensive antics of a few of the newcomers around here made us feel like the original, crusty battle-tested veterans. The atmosphere was a little jumpy lately, because the helicopter squadron across the road had been mortared last week.

One of the new anesthesiologists who had become a real case study in paranoia had even been wearing his helmet and flak jacket into the operating room. A few days ago in the middle of the night, one of the OR corpsmen on the way back from having more than a few beers with a buddy, thought it might be funny to throw some small rocks on the roof of this particular medical officer's hardback accompanied by shouts of "VC in the compound!" Within seconds a wild-eyed figure waving a .45 came flying out the door headed for the bunker nearby. The corpsmen, realizing they could easily be targeted as VC by John Wayne in green skivvy shorts, wisely decided to hit the deck in record time. Meanwhile, our heroic gas-passer calmed down enough to realize he wasn't going to have to make a last stand after all. Nevertheless, he decided to spend the rest of the night in the bunker.

I asked Don about the MEDCAP routine, and he told me that most of the same stops on the weekly circuit were still taking place. As in the past, we had at least one trip a week to Hue, plus two helicopter trips to coastal villages when choppers were available. Surprisingly he had been having difficulty recruiting GMOs for these trips, so I was more than happy to volunteer. Most of these locations seemed safe enough, and besides helping to pass the time, it gave us unusual opportunities to come in contact with a side of Vietnam that was not often seen and usually off limits to most Americans. As in the case of Mai and many other Vietnamese with whom I'd been personally involved, there was no question that we could really make a difference in their lives. Any session of triage after a couple of chopper loads of DMZ area casualties arrived left us drained, depressed, and filled with sadness at the necessity of having to do such a job. Working with the civilians, we were sometimes able to balance the mental effects of such devastating destruction by participating in some healing and constructive treatment which was good therapy for us as well as our patients.

However, promoting the benefits of MEDCAP to prospective recruits had always been a challenge. We had to be sure to emphasize such extra attractions as fascinating sightseeing, fine local cuisine (true occasionally, but depended on the tolerance of the individual's intestinal tract), and exotic Vietnamese women (generally fantasy). Reminiscing about the whole subject brought back many memories of our first days on the MEDCAP trail.

"Have you seen the Colonel lately?" Don asked me. "I spent a few hours with him recently," I replied, "and the guy is living in a style befitting a southern gentleman with the 3rd Engineers near Da Nang."

The "Colonel" was strictly an honorary term, but appropriate for Dan Haverhill, a Mississippian who was a rebel to the very core. He was one of our toughest cases when it came to MEDCAP recruiting as he wasn't exactly enamored by anything Vietnamese. Mention of the Colonel and MEDCAP couldn't go far without bringing up the story of the ice cream parlor in Hue.

Of our different destinations, Imperial Hue was a highlight trip and usually not a hard sell when it came to getting volunteers. First of all, it was very scenic, sitting in a certain decaying colonial and historical elegance astride the Song Huong Giang or River of Perfumes. On the north side was the famous Citadel, enclosing almost two square miles within its walls, moats, and ramps as well as the inner walled conclave of the Imperial City, with its palace buildings, gates, lotus pools, and gardens. West of the Citadel just up from the river banks, was the 360-year-old Linh Mu pagoda. To the east was the sprawling open market enclosure and commercial center. On the opposite side of the river was the high school and university, a large provincial hospital, and various governmental buildings along with a residential district of spacious stucco villas that spoke of another era.

Being an off-limits, official-business-only area, Hue was also very Vietnamese. Except for the army MACV (Military Assistance Command Vietnam) compound plus military police, the U.S. military presence was minimal. Unfortunately, that situation was going to change drastically in a short time, but in 1967, Americans were a relatively uncommon sight in the city. Finally, our work there usually was pretty easy so that opportunities for side trips and sightseeing were ample. Throw in Hue's reputation for having the most beautiful women in Vietnam, and it was hard to see why we didn't have long lines eager to offer their services.

So it was that we prevailed on the Colonel to join our tour group for the run to Hue. Besides Colonel Dan, Don and I, our party included John Dobbins, our MEDCAP corpsman and veteran Hue tour guide, and Kelly, our interpreter. Kelly, who had spent a year in the U.S., lived in Hue and was pretty reliable and helpful, although he tended to get impatient with our customers at times. He often looked like a Saigon hood when he wore his patent-leather hat and sunglasses. Grabbing combat essentials like cameras, we piled into our jeep and one crackerbox (a panel truck that contained our medical gear) and headed for town.

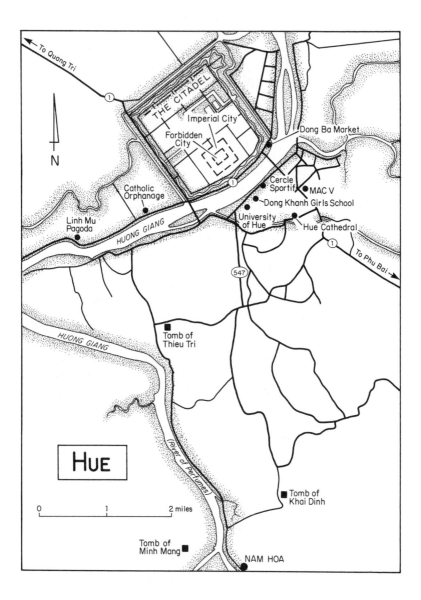

To Quang Tri

N

THE CITADEL

Imperial City

Forbidden
City

Dong Ba Market

Cercle
Sportif

MAC V

Dong Khanh Girls School

Catholic
Orphanage

University
of Hue

Linh Mu
Pagoda

HUONG GIANG

Hue Cathedral

To Phu Bai

547

HUONG GIANG

Tomb of
Thieu Tri

Hue

(River of Perfumes)

0   1   2 miles

Tomb of
Khai Dinh

Tomb of
Minh Mang

NAM HOA

A ramshackle refugee village, several ARVN outposts with sandbagged walls topped by rolls of barbed wire, thatched houses with an occasional fairly elaborate family tomb visible in the tree line across green rice paddies, young boys riding water buffaloes, and small buses with bicycles and baskets tied to the roof and overflowing with people— all were part of the passing scenery as we rolled down Highway 1 toward Hue. Near the outskirts was the incongruous sight of the massive grey-stone, red-roofed Hue cathedral dominating the view to the west. Soon we were driving across the main steel-girded bridge across the River of Perfumes, so named for the sweet-scented trees along its banks. Sampans of various sizes and other river craft drifted by, headed toward the market.

The Colonel was impressed. "Looks almost civilized," he snorted.

Next stop was the Catholic orphanage located a short distance off a one-water-buffalo wide street in a conclave of old, well-maintained buildings not far from the Citadel. As we arrived, a crowd of giggling and curious kids quickly surrounded us as we carried our two large boxes of totally unorganized supplies inside. Dobbins was especially valuable because he was the only person who could find things among the piles of pill bottles, bandage materials, assorted instruments, and bottles of disinfectant and cough syrup.

We usually held our sick-call in a small room adjacent to the main nursery. A glance inside would be returned by staring, mournful wide-eyed infants sitting in old metal cribs that looked like shopping carts. The sisters generally did a good job of bringing in the sick and not just the curious to be examined, and we saw only about 25 kids. Most of the problems were relatively minor, such as draining ears and skin infections, and easily dispatched. Then an orphanage tradition followed: A smiling younger sister brought us a tray of "lemonade" and cookies. I thought it was a cold kind of soft drink the first time, and after gulping down two glasses to please our hosts, I began to realize that our "lemonade" was really a kind of rice wine and good for a mild buzz. The Colonel appeared pleased and wanted to know if this kind of treatment was standard.

We then broke out cameras and took a brief walk around. Just as Father Matthieu, the sisters here were not reluctant to press for as much help as possible. At the same time, many of the 500 or so orphanage residents did a lot to help themselves. We saw young boys using ancient noisy looms, and fine silk embroidery work being done by some of the girls. Older people worked on pottery and carpentry items destined for the local market. As we strolled toward the sunny courtyard in front of the chapel, the head nun, Sister Isabelle, asked me if our friend was really a Colonel. I laughed and told her it was kind of an honorary title as he was from a famous southern family. She smiled, but looked a little puzzled as we assembled some volunteers with little difficulty for a picture-taking session.

We left the orphanage and stopped for a short time to try out my new movie camera, filming some scenes inside the Imperial City. The Emperor Gia Long's masterpiece of the early 19th century actually included not only the main Citadel and smaller enclosure of the Imperial City but also the innermost Forbidden City, which was reserved for the exclusive use of the Emperor and his family. Much of the Forbidden City had been ransacked during the war with the French. However, the yellow and green enameled tile roofs and columned halls of the temple of the Imperial City were in quite good condition and as yet unscathed by the current struggle. That would change dramatically during the Tet offensive of 1968 as the Citadel was engulfed in 25 days of some of the fiercest fighting of the war. For us, though, the quiet courtyards, peaceful lotus pools, and imposing roof-top ceramic dragons gave us glimpses of the grandeur of the past. Of special interest were the three side-by-side gates with ornate crests. The center gate was the highest, and according to Kelly, for the use of the Emperor alone, certainly not for a lowly *bac-si* or even a Colonel. Instead of mandarins, there were only a few caretakers around plus some Vietnamese boy scouts practicing some formations. Otherwise we were the only other visitors to be seen, and of course we were on official business.

A few minutes from the Citadel was Loc Thanh, our favorite spot for local cuisine. We climbed up the stairs to the bright, airy second-floor restaurant and were soon awaiting the usual four-course light lunch while cooling off with some Bia La Rue or Tiger beer. Eating here often seemed to result in a few extra trips to the Medical Library during the next 24 hours, but I always felt it was a risk well worth taking. Our meal consisted of *pho* (a tasty noodle soup with bean sprouts and small strips of meat), delicious shrimp, a chicken and vegetable dish, and bananas for dessert. For the adventurous, there was the ever-present *nuoc mam,* or fermented fish sauce, for seasoning on the side. The Colonel, strictly a "meat and potatoes" man, couldn't get too excited about the menu and settled for beer and a few shrimp. Colonel Dan was a good man in general and a solid physician, but when it came to appreciating the merits of Asian culture, he had a hard time. I had never known anybody very well who was born and bred in the deep south, and in some areas his view of the world definitely included some stereotypical prejudices that were hard to ignore.

Anyway, his mood brightened somewhat when Kelly suggested a visit to a genuine Vietnamese ice cream parlor not far from us.

We parked in front of a small shop located on a side street across from the market along one of the canals that crisscrossed the city. Inside it was cool and nearly deserted. We ended up with a kind of sherbet that tasted mostly like coconut and wasn't bad at all. Perhaps in honor of his western customers, the proprietor played an old Elvis record on his less than state-of-the-art record player behind the counter. After a pause, the next selection turned out to be, of all things, a scratchy recording of none other than Dixie.

The Colonel let out a yell. "Hey, these boys really have good taste in music," he said, breaking out in a huge smile. He was in hog heaven. There was no doubt about it. "Kelly," the Colonel roared. "I've got 200 piastres here for that boy. Tell him just to keep playing that record until I say to quit."

Kelly couldn't believe he wanted to hear it again, let alone pay for it.

"Dien cai dau" (crazy), he shrugged. We ordered another round of ice cream while the Colonel sat back and dreamed of the good life back home.

On the way back, Dan's view of Vietnam had at least temporarily improved. He didn't even mind too much an afternoon spent with the customary swarms of people at Loc Ban, a small village south of Phu Bai, where we often were overrun with patients and spectators. Subsequently, anytime we made an appearance at the ice cream parlor, Dixie was automatic for awhile, even if the Colonel was not along. Hue would surely be treated kindly in Dan's account to the home folks.

As our bull session continued far into the late hours of the night, Don told me that not only had the ice cream parlor closed up, but also Lac Thanh was no longer open either for some reason. On that kind of down note, I stretched out in my cot and wondered what the remaining eight weeks would add to our collection of the year's best war stories.

That weekend, we had an opportunity to pay a social visit to Hue. The Chinese embassy was having some kind of an anniversary reception, and because of our MEDCAP activities, we had been invited. Because of security problems on Highway 1 after dark, we would spend the night at MACV and return in the morning. Later in the afternoon, we drove into the MACV compound, which was actually a converted three-story hotel protected by a high brick wall. As I was getting out of the jeep, I noticed a familiar Vietnamese face among a small group of women heading for the gate. It was Hoang Hai, my former Vietnamese tutor from early A-Med days. She saw me and paused. Explaining that I had some official business to attend to, I left our group and walked over to say hello.

I had first met her when she brought her nephew to A-Med during my first month there last summer. He was on crutches with a painful swollen knee, the burned out result of some type of devastating joint infection. The Hue doctors had said there was nothing they could do for the boy and suggested taking him to the Americans.

Hoang Hai was slim and very attractive with long, dark hair, so naturally I couldn't resist an attempt to get to know her better. She was 19, a Hue university student and came from a fairly wealthy Catholic family that had originally fled from the Communists in Hanoi in 1956. It turned out that she had helped teach English to some fortunate army advisors at MACV, and so I tried to make some similar arrangements. Our orthopedist was in Hawaii on R & R, so after examining the boy, I worked out a plan for another visit in a week.

Subsequently, Hoang Hai and I spent some pleasant hours together and even if my Vietnamese didn't improve too much, I learned a lot about their life in Hue and her views about what was happening to her country. She was very afraid that they would become refugees again and greatly feared the Communists.

"Your country is so powerful and rich," she said, "and we are so poor. I think we don't survive unless you can help us more."

She was very proper, and her traditional family upbringing dictated even against having her picture taken by other than relatives.

I was able to obtain a new stethoscope for her older brother, a medical student, and she invited me to meet her family. That sounded like a good idea to me but presented some problems that I hadn't been able to solve earlier. Paying social calls to Hue civilians wasn't exactly standard operating procedure even for medical officers who were playing fast and loose with official regulations.

Talking briefly to her now, I told her I was going to be back at Phu Bai for awhile. She smiled and said, "I hope your Vietnamese is well," and wrote down an address, 10 Nguyen Tri Phuong Street, inviting me once again to visit. Her friends were waiting outside the gate, and she hurried off to join them. Watching her go, I thought about how unlikely it was for me to even meet a girl of her class. It wasn't hard to fantasize about what it might have been like under other circumstances, but for me at the present time, she was friendly, yet as remote as the daughter of a mandarin in the court of the Emperor.

After looking around for a short time, I found Don unpacking his musty khakis in our palatial quarters for the night. Real beds, hot and cold running water, even a genuine flush toilet—we had joined the wrong branch of the service. Scraping the mildew off my shoes, I was ready for the reception which was going to be held at the Cercle Sportif, the old French sports club. Driving over, we were treated to the sight of a Hue-style rush hour: a steady procession of long-haired high school girls on bicycles, white *ao dai* fluttering behind them. "Like butterflies on wheels," I had heard someone say. The Dong Khanh High School, one of the most prestigious schools for girls in Vietnam, was nearby, and I made a mental note to look into generating an excuse to check out the medical facilities there.

The reception was taking place on the veranda of the Cercle Sportif, built out over the banks of the river. The view from there was worth the trip by itself. Shadowy sampans made their way slowly downstream under a darkening sky filled with golden tinged clouds. We walked around and shook a lot of hands in a moderate-sized crowd of Chinese, assorted American military, USAID people, and Vietnamese officials. I spent some time talking to a couple of German physicians who had been teachers at the Hue medical school for over five years. They said they were so used to the war and various rumors of Communist threats that they didn't worry about it too much any more. We sampled some fairly potent drinks, I think it was cognac, and had fish and cheese on stale Ritz crackers. The affair wasn't exactly elegant, but it was an interesting diversion and change of pace from the usual routine. We returned to MACV in time for some late dinner and took in a showing of Rio Concho, a fairly decent western which we watched in its entirety on a wide screen with no film or projection breakdowns. We slept between the sheets that night before returning to the real world in the morning.

One week later, another unexpected chance to go to Hue arose. One of the army advisors wanted to discuss the possibility of a new MEDCAP site west of the city. Since I wasn't on call that Saturday, I jumped at the chance to keep Don company, and we also decided to sneak in a market stop afterwards. Don also wanted to look up another army friend at MACV so it dawned on me that perhaps I had an opportunity to work out a social visit of my own. All I needed was some transportation, and fortunately our driver for the day was PFC Washburn, a short-timer late of the 2/4 motorpool. I knew him well from our battalion MEDCAP days so he was not opposed to stretching regulations a bit for a good cause.

"Have a good time, doc," he said leering at me, "and don't smash up my jeep."

Hoang Hai's house turned out to be only five minutes away and easily located. I parked in an inconspicuous place and walked up a sunny driveway flanked by stands of bamboo and a large banyan tree to a house built in the French colonial style. My knock on the door was answered by an elderly servant woman who puzzled over my halting Vietnamese. Then I heard Hoang Hai's voice from the room beyond. I was ushered into a large, cool, rather dark room, where, strangely, most of the furniture was covered up and the appearance was that of an impending move. Hoang Hai was wearing black silk pants and a simple white blouse. She looked more like a peasant girl from Dai Loc than the fashionably attired Vietnamese lady I had always known before. She then introduced me to her parents, and we sat together around a low teakwood table as ice tea was served.

Answering my questioning look, she explained that they were in the process of building a large basement family bunker because of rumored NVA rocket and mortar attacks. Her father, who had been a Hanoi businessman originally, now was working for the RVN government, and he had become more concerned about their future in Hue because of recent threats, especially against anyone who had been associated with the Americans. He talked sadly about his fears that Hue, still hanging on as a mecca of Vietnamese culture, would be a prime Communist target. We talked for another 45 minutes or so when suddenly there was a knock on the door. I was called to the door expecting trouble, and I found it in the person of an impassive robot of an MP. I got nowhere with my best story about a medical follow-up visit, and reluctantly I was forced to excuse myself. With the friendly MP waiting like an eager predator in the driveway, Hoang Hai came to the door with me. There was little time for anything but a quick thank you and goodbye, and the door closed on what had been a very enjoyable morning interlude.

Later, driving back to Phu Bai, I thought about the torment of their life under the constant threat of war and the prospect of flight again from their second home. How unfair life could be! Weren't these people entitled to some peace and security in their lifetime?

Actually, the trip had been a pretty successful one overall, and my mood brightened as I thought of our souvenirs: two famous Hue conical hats apiece. Sandwiched between layers of a type of palm leaf material were delicate designs and even poems in fine colored paper which were clearly outlined when the hat was held up to the sun.

In addition, the new MEDCAP spot was a return to our old Nam Hoa village stop, which had been discontinued because of VC activity in the area. Located west of Hue along the river, about a thirty-minute drive away, it was of great interest to me because it was the region of many of the extravagant royal tombs of Vietnam's last dynasty of rulers.

We had talked often about possible ways to pull off a visit to the reportedly fabulous tombs of Gia Long and Minh Mang. These two were west of the river near the base of the mountains, but unless we could borrow a platoon of Marines and some helicopters, we would just have to speculate about the gardens and temples of their small cities of last repose. Also, supposedly these sites were VC and NVA sanctuaries, because the enemy felt they were immune from ARVN artillery or mortars due to the historical significance of the tombs. It was not the best place for some camera-toting medical officers to be found.

However, we had been able to get a look at the tomb of Thieu Tri (one of the 49 sons of Minh Mang), which was easily accessible from the road to Nam Hoa on the more friendly side of the river. His rule had been short, lasting only from 1841 to 1847, and perhaps for that reason his last resting place was relatively modest. The main buildings were hidden in the trees behind a walled enclosure where locked gates were pockmarked with bullet holes. In front was a courtyard guarded by near life-sized warriors and elephants of stone plus two large lotus-choked ponds where blue dragonflies hovered like tiny helicopters. Once on the way back from Nam Hoa, we had stopped for a picture-taking session as the warm light of late afternoon slanted across the courtyard. The serenity was broken by the sounds of explosions from an air strike in the foothills across the river. I took pictures of jets pounding away at hillside targets framed by the same three gates we had seen in the Citadel.

Don and I started scheming immediately and things started to fall into place. For our return trip to Nam Hoa, we looked more like an attack force than a bunch of medical non-combatants on a peaceful mission. We were led down the road by our Army counterpart in a jeep with a mounted .30 calibre machine gun, while a jeep with four Marines with M16s protected our rear. We were welcomed by a horde of patients in a lengthy morning session. Nothing seemed to have changed much in the village, which was near a ferry. The other side looked peaceful and tantalizing, but we decided it might be wise to settle for a visit to the tomb of Khai Dinh several kilometers west of us.

Khai Dinh died in 1925, the next to last in the line of 13 Nguyen

Emperors. Although he was a symbolic monarch only (the French having taken Hue in a bloody struggle in 1885), he played his ceremonial role well, with lavish celebrations in the Imperial City. It appeared, though, that he countered his relative impotence as a ruler by constructing a magnificent tomb, easily the most impressive I had seen. It was an imposing multilevel structure with a broad stairway going up to a large courtyard with a veritable army of stone guards standing at attention in silent formation along with elephants and horses. In the center was a central pavilion with a statue of the Emperor and a large bronze tablet telling of his glorious deeds. From the first terrace, wide flights of stairs flanked by slim, elaborately carved towers led upward to higher levels and the main building itself. It was possible to go inside a small but very elaborate anteroom chamber where locked doors prevented further exploration. In front of a very large, gilded carved cabinet stood a great urn and also a bronze crane resting on the back of a turtle. Later we found out that the crane and turtle symbolized longevity and hard work (neither of which seemed to apply to Khai Dinh), while the urn commemorated the Emperor's reign.

Outside, the view from the top level was really nice — contrasting green with rice paddies and banana trees and glimpses of the River of Perfumes through low rolling hills, with the jungle-clad screen of mountains as a backdrop. It was a tough place for any eager photographer with an itchy shutter finger to consider leaving in a rush. However, we were now in the somewhat somber shadow of a building cloudbank, and there was kind of an eerie stillness. I thought about the significance of Duc, our interpreter for the day, deciding to stay back in Nam Hoa. We decided not to push our luck, and, collecting our line troops from among the Emperor's stone legions, we headed back home, thankful that the VC had recognized us for the harmless non-combatants we were.

The following week we were asked to come to the Hue cathedral for a MEDCAP visit. We were more than happy to oblige, as the priests had been very nice to us. To accommodate our tourist impulses, they had once allowed us to climb up the bell tower to a Quasimodo perch with a spectacular viewpoint. There was a pretty big crowd, and we found ourselves busier than expected. I was in the midst of an incision and drainage procedure on a screaming two-year-old who had a huge abscess in the left chest area. As I was reaching over to fill up my syringe with saline for more irrigation, I suddenly spotted Hoang Hai on the edge of the onlookers.

She looked rushed and anxious to talk to me. But I had my hands full, dealing with what seemed like quarts of accumulated pus in the loose soft tissue, so it took me another ten minutes to finish up. I rushed out through the crowd expecting her to be waiting, but Hoang Hai was nowhere to be seen. I waited outside for awhile, but she did not return. I had no idea at the time, but that was to be the last time I would see her. Later, when she didn't come to A-Med for more language lessons as we had planned, I recruited Kelly to do some detective work for me. He would only say that the house seemed locked up, and suggested that maybe he could arrange a moonlight sampan ride for me so I would feel better. What was going on that day? Why didn't she wait? I tried not to think of some of the bad things that might have happened. Maybe they just decided to leave the city. The mystery would be solved in the following year.

Catholic orphanage, Hue.

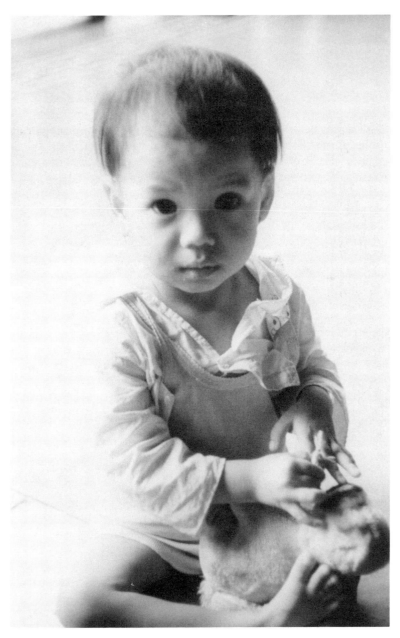

Catholic orphanage child, Hue.

Boys and looms. Catholic orphanage.

Emperor's gate, Hue citadel.

Thieu Tri's tomb outside Hue.

Local children on stone horse at entrance to
Thieu Tri's tomb.

Steps leading up to Khai Dinh's tomb near Nam Hoa.

Main building. Khai Dinh's tomb.

Perfume River, Hue.

CHAPTER SIX

R & R

Of all the many abbreviations in the panoply of military alphabet soup, R & R, or Rest and Recreation, was of course everybody's favorite. CONUS (Continental U.S.) was high on the list, too, because of its tour-ending association, but it was R & R that was the subject of many long hootch sessions and the ever-present fantasy for all of us. For some it meant a quick taste of an exotic Asian city or perhaps a second honeymoon with a spouse in Hawaii. For others it was a short return to sanity from the insanity of combat, which would be spent enjoying all the sensual delights that could be packed into five days.

Not infrequently the result would be a trip to the BAS right after returning for two generous injections of long-acting penicillin plus ten days worth of pills. For some Marines such a treatment came as a relief. One of our battalion senior corpsmen specialized in giving newcomers a lecture about venereal disease. He would conclude his little talk with a discussion of the need for more radical treatment for resistant cases. He then would produce what appeared to be a large, stainless steel corkscrew which he said was a special "surgical" instrument which was needed for a cure. The effect on his audience was predictable, at least for the short term.

R & R was theoretically available after three months in-country, and every one was entitled to make two five-day trips during the year. However, like anything else in the military, there was the official by-the-book way to do things and the unofficial under-the-table approach. When it came to obtaining an R & R billet, wheeler dealers and rear area people who specialized in working the system were in their element. There were some who managed to end up with three or even four R & R trips, not to mention an occasional in-country R & R weekend at China Beach in Da Nang.

The prize trips were those to Hong Kong or Bangkok, with other destinations like Singapore, Taipei, and Japan being less popular. Approval for R & R needed to go through the individual's commanding officer, and to a certain extent it was dependent on the unit's activity and location. So in actual practice, even though you were up for R & R, it wasn't always possible to go when or where you wanted. Unfortunately, sometimes the front-line people who needed the break the most had the greatest difficulty because of logistical hangups. Each unit had only so many allotted billets to each location. If nothing was available to Bangkok, for example, your choice was to settle for somewhere else like Singapore, or try again later. It could definitely get frustrating, and knowing somebody on the inside or having connections often paid off handsomely.

In my own case it took me ten months to make my first trip, and even then it was up in the air until the last minute. Naturally I was after one of the big two, and neither Hong Kong nor Bangkok seemed to be available at the right time. Finally I went the standby route, which meant a trip to the Da Nang R & R center without knowing if I would end up turning around with hopes dashed. It was an endless wait, but as things turned out, I got lucky and made the magical manifest for that day's flight to Hong Kong. We literally charged on board the chartered Pan Am DC-6B when the time came. Inside it was cool and comfortable. There were genuine round-eyed flight attendants passing out damp washcloths for us to sponge off some of the Da Nang red dust. It was pure luxury settling back in the seat and watching the familiar sights of Vietnam slip away. Our aircraft was no smooth, quiet 707 jet either, but the constant vibration from the engine was music to our ears at that point. Ahead, only around three hours away, was one of the most fascinating cities in Asia. It was very easy to shift gears and drift off with thoughts of exotic sights, fantastic food, hot showers, and of course Suzie Wong and her friends waiting for us at the airport.

Awakening as our plane started a rather bumpy descent, I looked out to find our view obscured by lots of light-grey cumulus clouds. In a short time we broke through at a lower altitude and had our first glimpse of the famous colony. Most striking was the obvious contrast between the crowded, poor areas, and the ultramodern buildings and hotels that marked the downtown areas of Kowloon on the mainland and Hong Kong Island. The bumpy hills of the Nine Dragons (Kowloon in Cantonese) were there in the background. I spotted the landmark high point of Victoria Peak on the island side. We cruised in lower toward Kai Tak airport, which jutted out into the harbor like a huge aircraft carrier.

As we descended I could see blocks and blocks of tenement high rises. Space was obviously at a premium here, as everything seemed to be built straight up. Each building was decorated with row upon row of family laundry hanging from every balcony. Squashed between these concrete block houses were narrow streets; some seemed just big enough for pedestrians. Here and there milling crowds of people could be seen in a market place. As we neared our destination, the streets became wider, and the buildings soared higher and appeared more luxurious. The scene could have been from any large city in the U.S. except for some incongruities, like huge, garish neon signs in Chinese characters. Some streets were jammed with vehicles of every description, and there was something strange going on—yes, that was it—everybody was driving on the wrong side of the street!

A short time later I was walking through the plush air terminal soaking up the atmosphere, especially the pleasant sight of a stewardess contingent from several different intercontinental airlines. What planet had we come from, anyway? There seemed to be no way Vietnam could be such a short flight away. A brief tour bus ride through crowded streets confirmed my suspicion that a pedestrian's life might not be worth much around here. We ended up in a large, bare classroom of a not-so-royal British military base where we were given a briefing on the do's and don'ts of R & R in Hong Kong.

We quickly learned that we were easy marks for everyone from pickpockets to money changers. Con artists were everywhere, we were told, and some of these hustlers frequented hotel lobbies looking for their tourist or R & R victims. Working on a commission-only basis, these opportunists had a whole collection of great lines and guises. Some would pose as R & R official hosts, hotel employees, or tour company guides. A favorite tactic was to first find out your name and unit in advance. Then you would soon hear how someone else from your outfit had been directed to the bargain of his life.

Shopping turned out to be a challenge for a real pro, as bargaining was the order of the day. To pay the asking price was, needless to say, the sign of a rank amateur. Fortunately for us innocent, generous big spenders, the Navy had established a big display store on Hong Kong Island where many of the leading shops pushed their products. Prices were relatively standardized, so if we didn't choose to do business directly with wily Orientals on our own, we could spend our Hong Kong dollars there.

Next on the program was picking a hotel. If you were not on a budget, the choice would be difficult, as Hong Kong was the home of some of the most opulent hotels in the world. I had decided on sticking to the Kowloon side, which seemed to have more of everything, including crowds. We had been told that in the Shan Shiu Po district, it had been calculated that there were an incredible 150,400 people per square kilometer. I settled for a middle-of-the-road hotel with a high-class name, the President, which was within easy walking distance of the Star Ferry and transportation to the island side for only Hong Kong $0.25 (HK $1 = 0.18$ U.S.). The hotel itself cost HK $40 per night. The price was definitely right and was good for a real nice air-conditioned double room with some other vital items like running hot water. I luxuriated in the pure pleasure of a long hot bath, so much more appreciated after all those brief, cold Vietnamese showers.

I had an afternoon left to get my bearings, so after shaking some of the mildew out of my civilian clothes, I headed for the street. I soon was lost in a world of Oriental exotica and commercial enterprise brought about by the successful 125-year marriage between East and West. The sights, sounds, and smells of Asia were there along with bustling capitalism in one of the world's most eye-catching bazaars. Looking for photo opportunities from a rooftop restaurant, I sneaked into the venerable Peninsula Hotel past a tall, bearded and turbaned Sikh who patrolled the entrance. However, I quickly felt out of place in the gilded palatial interior. Back to people watching on the street, I thought as I went back outside toward some non-stop entertainment provided by a grinning wok chef at work. Although I had eaten earlier, I got hungry again in a hurry and wasted no time finishing off a bowl of chicken, vegetables, and rice local-style.

A visit to the vast, airy ocean terminal was next on the itinerary. Passenger liners and freighters were double-parked along the huge multi-levelled structure. I wandered through a giant shopping mall with a maze of arcades and small shops which had a dazzling array of products that seemed to come from every corner of the world. Stopping off in a place called the Rice Bowl Cafe for a Coke, I went over all the possibilities for the next four days. A whole assortment of tours was available that ranged from Kowloon at night including some Chinese opera to a visit to the New Territories here on the peninsula with a glimpse of mainland China. Tomorrow I had to find a shop called the Mandarin Arts Company where my aunt in Oakland had been doing her Hong Kong catalog shopping for many years. Naturally she had sent me a shopping list and had even written written them to say I might be coming.

It was time for a late-afternoon ferry trip to Hong Kong Island. The green and white Star Ferry was crowded with passengers—a lot of Chinese businessmen in Western attire, some elderly Chinese women in their black pajama-style suits, locals reading racing forms plus an assortment of tourists. Looking at the predominately well-to-do crowd, it was hard to believe that just a short distance inland was the poverty and at times the terror of Red China. I decided to try out the Hilton's restaurant on the twenty-fifth floor and take in the spectacular view of night-time Hong Kong and its harbor. I ended up in a bar called the Eagle's Nest, listening to an Army major talk about his adventures at the Royal Hong Kong Jockey Club followed by the unsuccessful pursuit of a tantalizing Chinese girl on the beach at Repulse Bay.

The following day turned out to be a memorable one filled with surprises, and not at all what I had expected as I set out to find the Mandarin Arts Company. I figured I would take care of this obligatory shopping stop first, and then be free to investigate other things, like the legendary 24-hour suit.

Looking like any one of the 5000 other shops I had seen, the Mandarin Arts Company turned out to be located in a small shopping mall not too far from my hotel. Mr. Chiu, the owner, rolled out the red carpet for me when I mentioned my aunt's name.

"Oh yes," he smiled broadly, "we have been expecting you. Your aunt is one of our best customers."

I wondered how many times a day he said that.

"I'll be most happy if you will join us for lunch as soon as my son arrives," he continued, "and afterwards I'd like you to meet my wife and daughter."

This shopping trip was getting more and more interesting I thought. With a special "discount" and such hospitality, how could I help but find a few more items to buy? Although unpretentious on the outside, to my uneducated but wary eyes, the shop seemed to have a lot of quality goods. It looked like I really couldn't go wrong here.

Our luncheon spot, the Imperial Rest, was a large second-floor restaurant frequented primarily by Chinese businessmen. I had the distinct impression that I was the only Westerner in the crowd. We were joined by two friends of Mr. Chiu, one of whom was a kind of evangelical Presbyterian preacher. Before we ate, he proceeded to say a very long prayer primarily devoted to my work in Vietnam, and hopes for a safe tour there. It was a very nice gesture, but I was sure that everyone was more than ready to eat by the time he concluded. How funny, I thought. Here I was, eating with Chinese in Hong Kong, and the meal was blessed by a Christian prayer that would have made the most ardent fundamentalist proud.

We were having a "tea lunch," which our host explained was a very popular style of eating. It was a sitting Chinese cafeteria where young girls would walk around with trays of thirty or forty different dishes. You would simply pick and choose from the great variety that passed by your table. My hosts were determined to have me try some of everything, of course, and most of the time I had no idea what I was eating. I did recognize a few things besides the white rice, such as small tasty shrimps with mushrooms, a kind of panfried dumpling, sauteed scallops in a black bean sauce, and crispy pieces of chicken with golden brown skin. From C-ration ham and limas or the standard chow-line Marine fare to this, I mused as I gorged. It did take a little extra effort, too, as I amused my new friends by trying to manipulate the ivory chopsticks. I never did figure out how they knew how much to pay as there was no bill nor menu with prices.

I decided on the way back that maybe I should try to buy a few more things before I left. Then Mr. Chiu explained that we were going to have some tea and lotus-seed pastries with his wife and daughter, whose name was Celeste. His two friends left, and we went to a small garden area in the back of another restaurant near his shop.

They were waiting for us at one of the tables. Mrs. Chiu was a small, soft-spoken woman neatly dressed in the customary Chinese high-necked dress. And Celeste? I couldn't believe it! She was a striking, dark-haired beauty with large expressive eyes. Surprisingly she was dressed in casual Western clothes. Even more unexpected was the discovery that she had just returned home on her spring break from college in the U.S. Would you believe also that she was attending the University of Washington in Seattle? Talk about coincidence, I marveled, as we mentioned familiar names and places. She even liked to go to Tai Tung, my favorite Chinatown hangout below the hospital. It turned out that there were four daughters and two sons in the family, and she was the youngest. I had expected a demure, unapproachable traditional young lady to admire from afar. Was this my lucky day or what? But she would be leaving soon to return to school. How could I possibly figure out a way to see her again?

It was time to leave, and I thanked Mr. and Mrs. Chiu again for their warm hospitality. As we walked out, I asked Celeste about the floating restaurants in Aberdeen. She said that when we got back to the shop she would ask her brother, who had a friend working part-time as a tour guide. Soon we were all saying good-bye, and I reluctantly picked up my packages and headed for the door.

Back in my room at the hotel, I was putting things away when I noticed a business card fall out of the bag along with the list of my purchases. Idly looking at the elaborate red script in English and Chinese characters on the front, I tossed it back in the bag. But when I did, I saw there was something written on the back. I picked it up again, turned it over, and did a double take when I saw:

Call me at 5— Celeste; and a number.

I was on a morning ferry watching the sun dance across the waves from the wake of the boat. Reflecting on yesterday's developments, my thoughts drifted back to that late afternoon phone call. My hopes for having Celeste as my personal tour guide for the rest of the time here had met up with a hard dose of the reality of the situation. All was not lost, however, as she was trying to arrange to meet me for a trip to Aberdeen on the day after tomorrow on a Lotus Tour junk, thanks to her brother's friend.

For now it was time to take a look at the merchandise on display at the Navy Purchasing Branch at the China Fleet Club. It was like a big trade show with representatives from many of the well-known stores manning booths with some of their products available there on the spot. Or, if you liked what you saw, you were provided with directions to the main store for more in-depth shopping. As I learned more, I found out that these companies had contracts with the U.S. government which supposedly guaranteed quality as well as discounts. We'll see about that!

Back to the 24-hour suit department, it seemed as though half the population were tailors, making a choice a real challenge. The Fair & Square Company and others like it I had already seen didn't inspire a lot of confidence about what might happen to your suit after the first trip to the cleaners. There were only six to choose from at the NPB so I went with the one that had the friendliest salesman and the best-sounding name.

Later, after a fitting at the Loa Hai Shing Company, I walked out after having dropped a fast 180 U.S. dollars. I had intended originally only to pick up a sports coat for myself and one for my dad. However, finding myself in what appeared to be Bargain City, I ended up getting three sports coats and four pairs of slacks. There were smiles all around, and I was told that anytime I needed some additions to my wardrobe, they would be happy to fix me up, as they would keep my vital statistics on file. This place had to be good because nothing would be ready for a full 48 hours!

The rest of the day was a kaleidoscope of travel-poster scenes. The Peak Tram with its panoramic view of the island and its harbor was a must, especially at only HK $ 0.60 each way. It was a serious steep incline, and as the funicular car lurched upward, I found myself hoping the heavy cable was as strong as it looked. On the way down, I really played the crazy tourist role as I tried hanging off the varnished slat seats for some unusual camera angles.

Later I saw the famous ladder streets, which were steep, narrow lanes with steps cut in them. I poked around one of the stomachs of Hong Kong—a fascinating public market where it was possible to buy every part of almost any animal, bird, or fish. There were pigheads hanging from hooks, pans of bloody brains, strings of fish, and live snakes. It was a long way from an air-conditioned Safeway back in the U.S.A. I rode a clanging old street car to one more must-see on the afternoon's list—the Wan Chai waterfront district of Suzie Wong fame, for goodness sake. Blaring stereos, mah jongg parlors, and noisy bars spoke of the non-stop night life which could still be found in this notorious sailors' playground.

Besides the streetcars, buses and taxis, there really were some genuine rickshaws around. Seeing my camera, one smiling driver helpfully posed for me, but then I was blistered by a string of curses in Chinese when I didn't hire him for a ride. I tried to dissolve into the teeming crowd, which was always a truly international one here. The majority of course were Chinese, some in traditional dress but many in Western clothes. In addition there were typical stiff-upper-lip Brits, camera- clad Japanese, sauntering Americans, and impassive, dark Indians. The whole setting was perfect for tales of mystery and intrigue.

I decided on one more Peak Tram ride. It was noticeably cooler on top, and there were drifting low clouds. Nevertheless, the nighttime view, especially of the harbor was dazzling. I finished the day off roaming the stalls and small shops of what was called the "Poor Man's Nightclub." Here you could find fast food Hong Kong style in a cornucopia of culinary delights cooked to order under bare lightbulbs. Well-fed and ready for another hot bath, I caught the ferry back to Kowloon, where tomorrow would bring a trip to the New Territories.

Leased from China in 1898, the New Territories represented most of the colony's actual land area. This region was thrown in later, along with Kowloon, after the original ceding of Hong Kong Island to Britain in 1841. At that time, the British had insisted that the Chinese provide them with a safe harbor for their merchant vessels.

From the front of a modern tour bus with a pert, uniformed female guide, we covered some sixty miles on our trip. Highlights included a stop on a hill overlooking the border between Hong Kong and mainland China. The countryside was quite dry and reminiscent of the foothills of Southern California. Vietnam was a lot more scenic, I decided. Also, we spent a fascinating hour and a half and got a little exercise, too, at the Temple of Ten Thousand Buddhas. A climb of 400 steps was required to reach the main temple where monks chanted, and the walls were filled with small statues of seated Buddha.

Our guide told us quite a bit about one of the colony's major problems—refugees. As one might expect, this small area was bursting at the seams with over four million people. Refugees from mainland China were not home free once they escaped the Communists. British authorities would often have to send them back instead of welcoming them, because basically there just wasn't enough room. There were shortages of food, water, and other natural resources but the most scarce item was space. Level ground was at a premium. Much hill-moving and leveling was necessary to provide locations for the resettlement apartment buildings which were springing up as fast as possible. Much of the water supply came from the land of "glorious Mao," and more reservoirs were being built to try to become less dependent on the whims of the Chairman. The big question about Hon Kong's future remained unanswered, and a lot of joss sticks will be burned to bring good fortune when the lease finally runs out in 1997.

The cool, dignified tones of The World Today on the BBC brought me back to life on this last full day in Hong Kong. I had to tie up all my loose shopping ends, not to mention to pay a return visit to my tailor. Those little errands, which included some prolonged post-office time for mailing off some packages, took up most of the morning. Later I took a short tour of Hong Kong Island and visited several nice view points, the best being Repulse Bay with its sandy beach. The low point was the much-heralded Tiger Balm gardens, which proved to be a lot of tired ceramic figures from the world of Chinese mythology. The place was built by a gentleman who made his fortune selling Tiger Balm, a snake-oil type cure-all.

As the warm, late afternoon light spread over the harbor, I waited by a booth on a pier where a battered sign advertised Sunset Dinner Cruise with Lotus Tours. I had received a message with directions, but no mention whether Celeste herself would be able to come. I had my doubts as I looked out over a harbor that seemed to be a continual rush hour of every imaginable kind of boat traffic. It was a mishmash of huge ships, tugs, pilot boats, sampans, junks, and other miscellaneous craft going in every direction at once. I watched a sleek grey wolf of a destroyer bear down on an ancient sailing junk with lateen sails and a red hammer-and-sickle flag. I never saw what happened next because suddenly there were voices behind me.

I turned around to find Celeste and a young man dressed neatly in blue slacks, white shirt, and tie. She smiled and mischievously asked me if I was waiting for the ferry. I tried unsuccessfully to act nonchalant as I heard myself make some inane reply. She looked terrific in a pale red cheongsam and mentioned something about not having much reason to wear her Chinese dresses back in Seattle. Inwardly I was shaking my head in disbelief at my good fortune. Maybe it was the Ten Thousand Buddhas, but any way you looked at it, I couldn't have picked a better way to end my all-too-brief adventure in Hong Kong.

We climbed on board our well-travelled junk to join a small group of people. They were all Australians with the exception of one somewhat loud Air Force captain from Saigon. Celeste and I found a spot on the forward deck away from the chug-chug of the engine, and we talked quietly as our boat slipped through the calmer waters away from the turbulence of the main harbor. The forty-five minutes to Aberdeen went quickly. Our conversation ran the gamut of topics from Vietnam to her growing up in this unique place. Going away to school was very common, and one of her brothers had preceded her to Seattle.

She told me that there was some anti-war stuff going on at the university. "But," she said as her expression hardened a little, "they have no idea what the Communists are really like."

She continued, "Do you know that some of the younger people here want to see the Nationalists invade China? They even want to volunteer to fight."

"That's pretty idealistic," I answered, "and a little crazy too."

She nodded in agreement as we watched our boat ease up to a rickety dock.

In a short time we found ourselves ferried in sampans out to one of the mammoth, brightly lit floating restaurants. All around us was a city of floating people, with thousands living on board their fishing junks and large sampans. Our destination, the Sea Palace Floating Restaurant, was a glittering spectacle of lights which outlined every dimension of the boat.

Once on board we had a chance to pick out our dinner selections from big tanks of fish and lobsters. I didn't know if we actually ended up eating what was netted for our approval, but it couldn't have tasted any better. The meal was outstanding, and we had a high-spirited, lively group. True to form, the Aussies began to get pretty wild as time went on. At that point I suggested to Celeste that we go up on the second level and find a quiet table for the two of us. She readily agreed, and we were soon sipping tea at a table near the railing, looking out over a carnival display of lights on the water below us.

I was enjoying myself thoroughly. Yet at the same time I was conscious of the sobering fact that there wasn't much sand left in the hourglass of our time together. Celeste was a real delight—one minute the exotic, mysterious daughter of a mandarin and then a bubbling, light-hearted modern university coed. I found myself thinking that I was beginning to get in pretty deep, and that the whole scene was beginning to look like something out of a novel. How was it all going to end up anyway, I wondered?

Maybe she was reading my mind because a moment later a more serious expression came over her face as she looked across at me.

"My father is sending a car for us. We'll drop you off at the ferry so you won't have to go on the tour van with the others."

As I gave her a questioning look, she went on, "You see, that was the only way he would allow me to go with you. He likes you and it helps that you are a doctor, but still you can guess what kind of a reputation American servicemen from Vietnam have."

So that's the way our little drama would conclude, I thought. I resolved to make every minute count, and we exchanged addresses while finishing a last cup of tea.

A short time later a vintage white Mercedes sedan pulled up along the pier where Celeste and I were watching a local dockside dice game. Mr. Chiu's modest store must have a lot of good customers, it appeared. We drove off, leaving the bright lights of Aberdeen behind us as we made our way back across the island. I couldn't get over the unreality of the situation. Tomorrow I'll be riding in some dusty jeep, I mused, and here I am with a chauffeur and a beautiful Chinese girl. Don't wake me up, I thought; I don't want it to be over. But then all of a sudden we were pulling up next to the Star Ferry Terminal. There was a light misty rain, and the bright lights around us were reflected off shiny mirrors on the surface of the pavement.

She said something in Chinese to the driver as we got out. We walked a short distance hand-in-hand and stopped near the entrance.

"You have to hurry because the last ferry is at 11:30," she cautioned me, "but at least it's not cold like Seattle."

Nothing could have been further from my thoughts at the moment.

I groped for something to say. "Thanks for a dream, Celeste." We shared a warm embrace and a lingering kiss.

"Be safe," she whispered, her eyes glistening a little. I kissed her quickly once more before she turned to hurry back to the car. She paused briefly at the door for a quick wave and then was gone.

Somewhere off in the distance, I heard a loud whistle as the curtain dropped on my own personal melodrama. Now for me, just like many others, the bittersweet ending to a five-day fantasy had arrived. I stared out across the water as the downtown lights of Hong Kong Island receded into a memory.

One minute we were standing in the futuristic Kai Tak terminal, and then a short nap later, we were back in good old Da Nang. I dozed off during the flight hearing comments like:

"I don't like American girls anymore."

"I don't care if I ever see another round eye."

"Hey man, if I don't get the clap, it won't be because I didn't try."

Upon arrival one slight, meek-looking Army PFC was greeted at the airfield by three MPs and a court martial. All he did was beat up some Hong Kong MPs, assault some civilians, and bring a loaded weapon into Hong Kong in his suitcase.

I spent three sweltering hours hanging around before I finally stepped into the cavernous mouth of the cargo door of a C-130 headed north to Phu Bai. I walked right into some real bad news in the A-Med triage area. I learned that one our 2/4 corpsmen had been brought in after surviving a booby trap which killed two Marines next to him outright. Subsequently there were major problems in the OR with bleeding, and despite everything that was done, in the end he just didn't make it. He was one of the most outstanding corpsman I had known in Vietnam—

bright, hardworking, and well-liked by all.

As the Chaplain used to say, I felt lower than a snake's belly. Welcome back to reality, *Bac-si*!

Corpsmen and friends.

CHAPTER SEVEN

Choppers

The pulsating beat of an approaching helicopter was a basic theme in the soundtrack of Vietnam, stimulating instant vivid recall years later for most veterans. Choppers provided unprecedented mobility, basic transportation, firepower, and salvation. They came in a wide variety of sizes and design—from small, glass-bubble observation craft and sleek Huey gunships bristling with machine guns and rocket pods to ungainly twin-engined Chinook transports and huge flying cranes. They were fascinating to watch, and I once spent some time at the airstrip during a late Dong Ha afternoon doing nothing but filming take-offs and landings. In particular, I featured a large transport craft which had its twin engines painted to look like huge, bulbous bloodshot eyes giving it the appearance of some kind of monstrous prehistoric insect. Most of the time helicopters brought us trouble and meant depressing hours dealing with the devastating effects of modern weapons. They also brought starched and squeaky-clean VIPs to the red, raw dirt of a forward combat base. And occasionally, when there wasn't much else for them to do, they brought doctors and corpsmen like us to otherwise inaccessible MEDCAP sites.

Our favorite airborne site was the junk fleet village about a thirty-minute flight south from Phu Bai. The coast between the mountainous Hai Van pass north of Da Nang and the sandy flat lands east of Phu Bai included two large bays that were nearly closed off at their entrances to form coastal lakes. The northernmost and largest of the two had a network of rivers and inland waterways at its upper end and long narrow coastal strips of land. At its tip near the tight entrance to the bay was one of the Vietnamese Navy's junk bases. Along over 1200 miles of coastline were many of these units, whose purpose was to try to prevent infiltration of men and supplies from the north. Each junk force had several motorized sailers or motorized rivercraft, and often an American advisor.

For us helicopter fanciers, the scenic ride to the junk fleet was worth the trip by itself. As an extra added attraction, we had the pleasant prospect of some beach time as well. That's right—a dip in the South China Sea was a regular feature of a hard day's work at the junk fleet. Loading our supplies onto the workhorse UH-34 Marine helicopters gave some clues to the fact that we weren't exactly a hard-core reconnaissance team heading for the mountains. Besides two big boxes of medical gear, an occasional case of beer plus swimming trunks and towels could be seen.

First priority when getting on board was a good position next to the open door, as having a prime photographic vantage point outweighed any risk of being a better target for VC marksmen. Then with the increasing chop-chop roar of the blades, the aircraft would start to lighten as it strained to be off. Following a short taxi, first the tail would lift off, and we would pick up speed as the rest of the chopper became airborne. Often the pilot would then rapidly gain altitude up to cruising level in an exhilarating series of steep circling banks. The door gunners, each with a mounted .30 calibre machine gun, would be especially watchful during take-offs and landings, even in relatively secure areas like the airfield at Phu Bai. The helmet I inherited when I first arrived belonged to a sergeant who had been hit by a round through the floor of a C-123 transport when taking off from Phu Bai for a flight to Da Nang. Fortunately, it was not a serious wound but it was literally a parting shot, as he was going south to catch his flight back to the U.S.A. at the time.

The view out the door past the menacing machine gun was really spectacular, and I had to be careful when rolling my movie camera. To be a casualty in Vietnam by falling out of a helicopter while taking pictures would definitely look bad. South of Phu Bai we first flew over flatland with rice paddies and small clusters of thatched houses. Visible also were strange groups of circular mounds which looked almost like graves. They were actually round strawstacks accumulated after rice harvest. As we neared the great glistening Cau Hai bay, it became more of a deltaland of partially flooded plains with the confluence of several rivers. West of the bay, the high spine of mountains rose up steeply and somewhere among the summit ridges was supposed to be a fabulous resort, an R & R spot for VC officers, so we had heard. As we flew over the eastern side of the bay, below us were a number of fish traps which were strikingly outlined and looked like huge arrowheads pointing toward the narrow opening to the sea.

As we neared our destination near the end of the coastal spit of land, we started to circle lower over a little islet just offshore, and a yellow-green, all-clear flare was set off. We settled down in a cloud of dust next to some huts and one hardback with a painted South Vietnamese flag on the roof that marked the quarters of our hosts. Nearby was a barbed-wire cage for VC, good for a picture with an imprisoned *bac-si* when empty. This particular village was pretty solidly anti-VC from what we'd heard, and the Navy lieutenant said he was fortunate to have some hard-nose Vietnamese sailors there. We saw several who had tattooed oaths to kill VC, instead of U.S.-style tattoos of dragons, women, or the occasional oddball like "sweet" and "sour" above the nipples on one older corpsman I had known.

We carefully negotiated the narrow one-plank bridge with our unwieldy metal boxes of supplies. Immediately we were surrounded by a big crowd of village children who would be our escort on the way to the schoolhouse where we generally worked. The mood was friendly, and the sun sparkled off the water of the bay. We walked past thatched huts, a marketplace, and an occasional small pagoda that looked out of place but picturesque in this spot—like ruins of some ancient temple in the midst of the jungle. On the shore side, fishing nets were stretched out to dry in the warm morning sun and villagers in their sampans watched our procession with a mixture of curiosity and indifference. Marching up to the school building, more children arrived yelling, "OK, OK", "Numbah One" and "Hallo, hallo." Spotting my camera, some of the bolder ones decided they were just the subject I'd been looking for, and I had my choice of many laughing faces accompanied by mock salutes. I photographed three nine-or ten-year-olds with their latest toy—some large dragonflies straining to escape their leash of fishing line.

Finally we got organized inside and in the next two hours or so, three perspiring *bac-sis* did their best to administer to the needs of 90-100 patients. Skin infections and boils were very frequent, and it was here that I had first become *Bac-si* Pus.

"Another one for *Bac-si* Pus," shouted Duc as he brought another unhappy youngster with a scalp crusted with sores and several ripe boils. How about a little soap once in awhile, we kept asking Duc and Kelly. They said it only cost 10 piastres, but whether we were up against unavailability or long-entrenched aversion to its use, it was difficult to understand. In the meantime, we passed out enough to turn the whole bay into a bath tub, along with some stern lecturing. Sometimes we had at least one Seabee dentist along who would have plenty of stoic customers lining up for extractions. Once to the great amusement of the spectators, I held some lip retractors so Jim Marks, the dentist, could take pictures of some betel-nut-stained sets of teeth for future slides for his colleagues back home.

Lunchtime finally arrived, and we walked back to the local Safeway to look for some items to supplement our tired ham sandwiches. How about bananas, some chunks of sugar cane and pineapple skewered on bamboo, and *ba muoi ba* or 33 beer (the other favorite local brew)? Next we boarded one of the junks for a short cruise to the ol' swimming hole—in this case a stretch of sandy beach on the seaward side of the narrow spit of land which narrowed the inlet of the bay. Our 46-foot craft was one of their motorized sailers with mounted .30 calibre machine guns and a garish baleful eye on the prow to ward off evil spirits. Soon we were diving overboard into the bathtub-temperature green water for a short swim to shore and a quick sprint over hot sand to the surf. Often some children from the village would meet us for some fun and games in the small waves. Was this vacation scene really somewhere in war-ravaged Vietnam? If it weren't for fleeting thoughts of the possibility of VC watching us from the hills across the inlet and the silent junk deck guns nearby, there was nothing at this scenic deserted beach to suggest a wartime existence. The irony of these moments was always present but yet easily overshadowed by such an invigorating and enjoyable change of pace.

Back at the junk base while waiting for the choppers to arrive, the medical officers had been known to get in some target practice. With encouragement from our hosts, we would put on an awesome display of pinpoint marksmanship with our .45 pistols as we blasted away at beer cans out in the water. Just like at Camp Pendleton, the damn things were so uncooperative and heavy that it was hard to imagine hitting anything on purpose unless at point-blank range. Usually these sessions ended by one of the sailors grabbing an M16 or grenade launcher and blowing the unscathed targets out of the water.

On return flights, the softer afternoon light made the view to the east of passing coastline and blue expanse of ocean especially nice. Naturally I'd run through a few rolls of movie film on that scene. Another favorite shot was down past my boot tops through the open door at the accompanying chopper (they always travelled in pairs) cruising along lazily below us. During this portion of the trip, the excitement and adventure of the day were past, and it was a time for reflection and relative quiet as we gazed at the now-familiar panorama spread out before us. At times we brought back not only the recollection of a pleasant day's trip, but also Vietnamese patients for treatment at A-Med or even some destined for the hospital ship *Repose*.

We had two hospital ships available in the vicinity most of the time. The *Repose*, AH-16, with a 560-bed capacity and a staff of around twenty-five medical officers, including every surgical specialty, had been offshore quite a bit when big combat operations had taken place along the DMZ. I'd heard a lot about the *Repose*, and since I was supposed to be in the Navy anyway, I had always been looking for an excuse to check it out during my first stint at A-Med. Finally that day came for Colonel Dan Haverhill and me.

We had lined up several Vietnamese patients for the Repose when time was available—one man from the junk base village with cataracts, two teenagers with probably post-polio contractures, and a four-year-old boy with cyanotic congenital heart disease. There wasn't much going on in the field at that particular time, so the A-Med commanding officers told the Colonel and me that the light was green for our belated ship duty debut. Eleven patients, one corpsman, and two eager medical officers were ready to go on a grey and blustery morning. However, because of some unexpected resupply runs, our flight was put on hold for awhile. Then, just as it began to look like a lost cause for the day, around 3 o'clock in the afternoon, we got the word that we might make it after all. Sure enough, a short time later, we were airborne for what was to be one of the year's most memorable chopper rides.

The *Repose* was lying off the coast of the DMZ so we headed north under overcast skies. Just past Hue, conditions started to deteriorate, and we found ourselves buffeted by stormy gusts and struggling forward into a grey void with no sign of land below. All of a sudden it was no longer a joy ride, but a wild, disoriented white-knuckle elevator trip. The Colonel's wide-eyed anxious expression mirrored my own as he mouthed a holy sh—against the roar. We sweated it out for another ten minutes, and then much to our great relief we were out in the clear with rain-soaked paddies once again visible below. It began to look like smooth sailing ahead as the clouds were lifting enough to give us some breathing room.

But the fun was just beginning. After passing Quang Tri, for some reason the pilot suddenly decided it was time to go down for a closer look. We dropped down rapidly as the door gunners swung their machine guns to the ready position. We zoomed along at treetop level startling farmers who looked up in surprise from their fields. What was the big idea anyway? The Colonel just shook his head and returned my totally baffled look. We swooped over a herd of water buffalo that promptly stampeded in panic. Then we began to follow the course of a river toward the sea, twisting and banking in a wild rollercoaster ride. I was half expecting to start receiving fire from each tree line around every bend. But there were only a few houses, an occasional small sampan, children playing in the shallows—the vignettes raced past. One more sharp turn between thick vegetation, and the river widened and lost itself in a sand flat delta. Ahead was our goal, a white toy ship with a red cross out on the grey sea. The chopper climbed steeply and reached a more comfortable altitude.

Why so low? It seemed reasonable that they would want to stay below the clouds, but they didn't have to practically land to do it. The flight had more the characteristics of a Huey gunship ride than a medevac flight. Maybe the pilot just wanted to give us a thrill or add a little excitement to a humdrum milk-run flight. Whatever the explanation, it was a memorable adrenaline rush of a ride that would not be forgotten. The boys in the helicopter squadron were going to have a few questions coming their way when we got back. The toy ship became larger, and soon we were settling down on the large, white crossed bull's-eye on the stern flight deck. We stumbled out and staggered out of the way, taking in the sights of the first ship of our Navy career. The other chopper landed, and the rest of the patients were taken off, including our Vietnamese who looked as completely lost in this alien world as we probably did. How different was the grey scrubbed atmosphere of a Navy ship compared to the sandbags and hardbacks of A-Med, not to mention the thatched huts and sampans of the junk base village.

We adjourned quickly to the luxury of the wardroom for some afternoon tea and coffee. "These guys are getting combat pay?" muttered the Colonel. Soon we landlubbers began to notice something else—the deck was not exactly level. In fact, we were pitching and rolling uncomfortably in moderately heavy seas whipped by high winds. We broke out the Dramamine, hoping stomachs hardened by fine Marine food would prove seaworthy as well. The *Repose*'s medical facilities proved to be as impressive as we had heard—several of the surgeons were quite enthusiastic about the idea of treating more Vietnamese patients when the casualty load was relatively light. At suppertime we dined in fantastic splendor—white tablecloths, fine silverware, delicious roast chicken, served of course on a silver platter, green salad, biscuits with honey, real milk, and ice cream for dessert. I quickly forgot my queasy stomach and decided the best approach was to fill it up. As for the Colonel, he was looking a little pale for a combat veteran, so we excused ourselves for a little fresh air. We went outside, leaned against the rail and stared out into the darkness, feeling like the original old salts. I decided right away that this life was what I had in mind when I signed up. Dan agreed but said he'd like it a lot better if the deck would hold still.

That night I slipped between the clean, white sheets of a spare upper bunk in one of the medical officers' rooms down in the depths of the ship. I settled back contemplating the day's adventures and sleep came quickly. Several hours later I was awake again, and I began to realize that my stomach was definitely not in good working order. The ship refused to move smoothly along and instead heaved and buckled as if it was personally trying to throw me out of bed. My first night at sea was not turning out too well, as I felt like I was on a trampoline going one way and my stomach the other. Give me back my nice, hard stable cot at Phu Bai, I thought, as I half fell down from the bunk searching desperately for some more Dramamine. Struggling back up and flopping down on my bunk, I tried to ignore the ship's gyrations by the fairly ridiculous method of counting helicopters taking off from a very flat and solid airfield. Somehow, after I got a squadron or two in the air, I managed to fall asleep before further disaster struck.

Morning came at last and the Colonel was yelling something in my ear about how great he was feeling and let's go hit the chow line. Unfortunately I was in no condition to even think of food and was barely able to get myself dressed without having to make a headlong rush for the head. Dragging myself up the imposing series of vertical ladders that led to the light of day, I found the *Repose* riding quietly in Da Nang harbor and behaving much more sensibly. It was a bleak, rainy day with low clouds obscuring all but the closest ships. Two fishing sampans propelled by long gondola-style oars creaked past us, followed by two men in a strange craft that looked like a very large floating basket. A rusting barge with a battered tin roof shack in the stern chugged toward a landing somewhere off in the mist. Soon helicopters began to ferry patients back and forth to NSA hospital, and it was time for us Marines to hit the beach.

Collecting the Colonel, who was thinking stowaway at that point, we jumped on the first available chopper. We spent some time in the air-conditioned Quonsets of NSA visiting some 2/4 Marines who had recently passed through A-Med. Then it was off to Marine Air Freight and a long wait watching the rain fall in sheets before eventually catching a very bumpy C-123 ride up to Phu Bai. Later that night, my appetite having returned over grease burgers and Kool Aid, we reminisced about the taste of the good life of an officer and gentleman aboard ship. And the mystery of our unexpectedly exciting chopper flight was solved. In possibly unfriendly territory, the pilots liked to make it a little harder for enemy gunners to zero in by flying lower, thus presenting a much faster moving target. There seemed to be some logic to it, but we decided in retrospect that it was kind of nice not to have known that flying the gauntlet was part of that particular flight plan.

Another very memorable helicopter ride was yet to take place. I was lying in the sun out in back of our hootch when Larry West, the orthopedist who was the CO of our medical battalion at that time, paid me a visit. He told me he was looking for a volunteer to go up to Khe Sanh to relieve a fellow GMO, George Rosen, who was up for a long-delayed R & R trip. Once again I couldn't resist a chance to spend some time at a place I'd always wanted to see, even though being officially a short-timer, it was probably wiser not to volunteer for anything. But on the other hand, George was a good friend, so I told Larry he'd found his man. I thought I'd catch a flight up the next morning, but just before dinner I got the word from the squadron that there were a couple of Huey gunships leaving for Khe Sanh in about 25 minutes. I jumped at the chance for a ride in one of those sleek, fast ships, so, figuring I'd only be there for at most a week, I threw some stuff in a bag and sprinted for the airfield.

I arrived sweat-soaked in time to find out, of course, that we wouldn't be leaving for another hour. I had hopes of adding another couple of rolls of footage to my helicopter movie collection, but it kept getting later and later. Finally at dusk, we were off in two Huey gunships armed to the teeth, each with two rocket pods, six mounted machine guns, and two door gunners with their M60 machine guns. The first part of the trip was similar to the flight to the *Repose*, only better, as we zoomed and banked just above the trees among the sand flats and paddies north of Phu Bai. The maneuverability and the speed of the UH-1B made our medevac craft look like lumbering air buses in comparison. Climbing steeply to about 1000 feet, we then cruised parallel to Highway 1, which could still be easily picked out as it led through the darkened countryside toward the lights of Hue. It was getting pretty dark at that point, and a few stars were visible over the coast while inland a dark curtain of clouds extended northward over the mountains. Suddenly we went into a screaming dive down to treetop level again. It was a real rollercoaster descent, and I began thinking we might be really in trouble as I noticed all the gauges on the instrument panel glowing a dull red. I started breathing again as we leveled off, and it dawned on me that the red glow was only to illuminate the dials at night. In a few minutes we gradually climbed up again, passing over the twinkling pinnacle towers of the Voice of America antennas. Then Hue was below us, and I picked out familiar landmarks— the cathedral, the river with its two bridges, the market, the striking walls of the Citadel—all still distinguishable as if in a giant relief map.

Passing Hue, we began flying over a mysterious grey-black expanse of flatland and paddies with only an occasional faint glow from some farmer's house breaking the darkness. What was Charlie up to down there, I thought as I looked over to the east and the few scattered lights that marked the Street Without Joy. The night certainly did seem to still belong to Victor Charles. It was easy to conjure up visions of black-pajama-clad men sitting quietly in the stillness plotting carefully another ambush or another way to bring their special brand of terror to the countryside.

Our route then began to turn toward the dark, forbidding sky over the mountains to the northwest. Passing Quang Tri we flew almost directly west for awhile following the blinking red light of the other gunship ahead of us. Then something happened that I still haven't been able to explain. As I looked out the port door past the dark silhouette of the gunner, I saw a large brilliant complex of lights way off in the distance to the west. Checking my bearings, Quang Tri was still visible to the rear out the right hand door, and Hue was now far behind. What could I possibly be seeing? If everything was really as it appeared, this city-sized apparition was lying right in the middle of the mountains in the direction of Laos. I tried to point it out to the door gunner, but he didn't seem to understand and my voice was lost in the roar of the wind and the engine. A Laotian city? A busy night on the Ho Chi Minh Trail? I was still trying to make some sense of it when we were swallowed up in the clouds.

There was an occasional variation in the darkness that seemed to indicate a mountain peak but overall visibility was not exactly optimal. I stared anxiously into the void trying to find something reassuring. At that point I had to admit I wouldn't have felt bad at all if the pilot had decided to turn back. He flew on though, undaunted, and casually lit a cigarette, flicking the ashes out the window into the fine rain that was now falling. The co-pilot was peering at his map with a flashlight. Ahead there was nothing but the red light of our companion plus an occasional flare somewhere in the foothills to starboard. It was a little strange looking down to see these flares instead of the customary view upwards to watch them twist to earth. I tried to dismiss thoughts of NVA gunners sitting around just waiting for a helpless bird to come by in the night, knowing that even if we weren't completely blown away, our chances of surviving a landing were about as good as my being promoted to admiral tomorrow. I also began noticing some flashes and the distant hollow boom of artillery fire. It sure would be nice if they know we're up here, I thought.

However, things started looking better a few minutes later when the starboard gunner leaned over and yelled at me that we'd be there in five minutes. We were travelling at around 3,500 feet as best as I could tell from my amateurish reading of the altimeter. Slowly we began to descend. Five minutes came and went and just as I was beginning to wonder again, suddenly there it was, the most welcome sight of the brightly-lit Khe Sanh airstrip. I halfway expected it to be completely blacked out in view of recent NVA rocket attacks, but the white and blue lights outlined it perfectly. Soon we were hovering a few feet above the ground as the pilot looked for a good place to set the ship down. It was a very relieved and excited *bac-si* that jumped out onto good, solid ground a few minutes later. This ride alone was worth the visit to Khe Sanh. There's no way I would have missed it, I thought smiling broadly to myself, especially now that we'd made it. Somehow I'd managed to try almost every form of helicopter transportation in Vietnam, from the giant, twin-engined Chinook transports to the top of the line Huey. Back home friends and family would have to suffer through movies and slides testifying to my fascination with choppers. Quite a switch for a basically sweaty-palm commercial airline passenger, I thought, as I stumbled off into the black night toward the only lighted tent I could see nearby.

En route to junk base. View from first class.

Junk base children.

Satisfied customer.

Medevac Sea Knight helicopter. Dong Ha airstrip.

CHAPTER EIGHT

Khe Sanh

I picked my way through some pallets on the side of the runway and walked toward the lighted tent. As I approached, it began to look as if I'd found the triage tent because there were some stretchers on supports silhouetted in one doorway. But as I drew closer, I realized something was wrong. A figure lying on one of the stretchers had an awkward, grotesque positioning of one arm. Instead of coming upon a tent prepared for caring for the living, I had stumbled on the tent that was used for preparing the dead for their final trip home. It was the Graves Registration tent. The whole depressing scene came into focus as I noticed a pile of dark green body bags inside the entrance. What an introduction to Khe Sanh, I thought, as I asked for directions to the A-Med Clearing Platoon.

The tendency was to become fatalistic about the prospect of death. Some Marines said you would never hear the sound of the incoming mortar round that would get you if it had your name on it. Since you would never know what hit you anyway, there wasn't much point in worrying about it. Sometimes it was just a question of being in the wrong place at the wrong time. The tragic story of my friend, the popular, good-natured sergeant from Samoa came to mind. He was accidently shot in the chest by one of his own men one night near Dai Loc while outside the perimeter checking on a position. The enthusiastic grin on his broad face while he was playing basketball in Okinawa with us in his bare feet will always be my favorite memory of him. And there were always stories about an individual whose number just wasn't up. I thought of the lance corporal who was brought to the BAS in Dong Ha because of a severe headache. The reason was pretty obvious when I took a look at his helmet, which had a massive dent. This fortunate Marine had been hit on the head by a mortar round that turned out to be a dud. Another story that made the local edition of the *Stars and Stripes* was the account of the PFC who saw the flash of a sniper's rifle and felt something strike him in the chest. Later when I examined him, I found a small contusion directly over his heart. His shirt pocket had a small hole and inside was the bullet. It was a "spent" round that had just barely made it to its target.

To keep your head down and not do anything stupid was a basic philosophy. I wondered whether volunteering to go to Khe Sanh might be categorized as showing questionable judgment for a short-timer.

Well, I thought woefully, it's too late for second guessing now—because here I am. I walked carefully in what I thought was the general direction. It was really dark. I rounded a sandbagged corner and spotted a red-and-yellow sign with the word Medevac. Thinking I was home free, I proceeded to fall into a trench at the back of what was apparently a volleyball court. I decided I didn't want to spend the rest of the night in the ditch. Fortunately not a casualty, I climbed out and made it the rest of the way to the next tent.

I walked in and Grant Garber stared at me for a moment from his cot. Finally I registered, and he exclaimed, "Hey, Rosen, look who's here." *Bac-si* Rosen was equally amazed, as he said he wasn't expecting anybody until tomorrow at the earliest. I filled them in on the highlights of a night chopper ride, and they pointed out the advantages of being in a bunker during a rocket attack. Their remarks were well verified by the presence of several ragged holes in the tent above Rosen's bed as well as by a large chunk of metal which Garber said he dug out of his pillow when he returned. There had been two KIA and ten WIA from the attack which had been with 122 mm rockets. Hey Charlie, I thought, that will be enough for now if you don't mind.

The rest of the night was quiet, and I awoke the next morning eager for a look around. After a tasty breakfast of C-ration hot chocolate, peaches, and toasted white bread, I swapped stories with Rosen about Bangkok for awhile. He was planning on some serious spending, and since this trip was his first R & R, I was sure he would.

"I'll see you in a week. Save me some C's.," he yelled as he grabbed his bag and headed for the airstrip. Taunts about what kind of souvenirs he was going to bring back followed him as he disappeared around the corner.

As for me, it was time to see what my latest vacation spot looked like in the daylight. The setting was certainly scenic and picturesque, just as I'd heard, particularly if you overlooked the conglomeration of dirty brown tents and bunkers of the combat base itself. Dark-green carpeted hills surrounded our mountain plateau location. Medium sized high cumulus clouds drifted by slowly in the light blue sky. The air was fresh and cooler at an elevation of 1500 feet. Immediately to the north of the airstrip the steep flanks of the highest mountains rose up—first in patches of light green high grass on the lower slopes and then the darker green of dense tree growth extending all the way to the ridgetops. Further away a series of hills extended away to the northwest. The summit of one of these hills was strikingly barren and brown. That had to be the infamous Hill 861, with its upper slopes already a devastated no-man's land from some vicious fighting.

A little below us to the east, Route 9 wound its way another eight miles past the villages of Khe Sanh and Lang Vei to the Laotian border. The airstrip itself looked like a great long mat of steel rug thrown down the center of the leveled-off dirt field. A C-130 transport roared off toward the coast. On board could be *Bac-si* Rosen, his eyes gleaming with thoughts of the exotic wonders of Bangkok. Three helicopters were warming up next to the west end of the runway getting ready for resupply runs to one of the hill outposts. Quite a few others were parked on the far side of the strip waiting behind steel barricades or revetments, which afforded some protection from incoming rounds. It was a little hard to imagine this one-by-two mile expanse of combat base as the small Special Forces camp it once was back in 1964.

With its proximity to Laos and its position only 18 miles south of the DMZ, Khe Sanh was felt to be an important strategic position by General Westmoreland. It was possible to block enemy infiltration along Route 9 and also utilize the airstrip for reconnaissance flights over the Ho Chi Minh Trail. However, there were logistical problems because of its remoteness, and these were much worse during the rainy season. In 1966, the Marines arrived, and the Special Forces unit moved to Lang Vei. The airstrip was lengthened, and the perimeter defenses were improved with rolls and rolls of barbed wire, claymore mines, and reinforced bunkers. Hills 861 and 881 south were occupied, and a radio relay installation was put in place on Hill 950 across from the airstrip. In return, as the war escalated, the Marines drew more attention from units of the NVA 325C division, which was well-equipped with artillery rockets and heavy mortars. Here it was possible to engage the enemy in more of a set-piece conventional battle instead of having to deal with the frustrating hit-and-run guerrilla tactics of the VC. On the other hand, some Marine Corps brass felt Khe Sanh was too much of a dig- in-and-wait defensive posture since the political climate seemed to have ruled out indefinitely an offensive drive into Laos against the Ho Chi Minh Trail.

From the medical standpoint, because of the type of fighting and the heavy weaponry of the main force NVA troops, more immediate triage support was necessary. Casualties were treated by us initially with additional assistance from the individual unit's people when things got really busy. Garber said it had been unpredictable recently with some slow days. As a result, he had time to devote to his pet project—the construction of his private custom hootch. "Emperors can build tombs," said the irrepressible Grant, "but I'm going to have my hootch." Built out in back of our tents from ammo boxes and leftover bunker construction lumber, it looked suspiciously like a 4-holer. It did have some real windows, though, and propped-open shutters that had just received a coat of red paint. He was currently bolstering its defenses and filling sandbags for a front door bunker.

"Any NVA who touches my hootch will have to answer personally to me," he shouted brandishing his Montagnard crossbow. Speaking of Montagnards, our neighbors here were mostly Bru tribespeople, as there weren't many lowland Vietnamese in the vicinity. MEDCAP had been limited to a rare foray down to the Special Forces Camp at Lang Vei.

Later that afternoon we got the ominous call that we would be getting some casualties from one of the companies up on the hill. At the same time we could see choppers hovering and flying around over a hill northwest of 861. In the meantime, the laid-back, casual pace of a lazy afternoon began to change considerably. The following scene was typical of the grim business of triaging casualties.

Stretcher supports were put in position, and IV bottles and tubing were set up. Blankets, splints, chest tubes, and dressing materials were readied. The various assignments of the corpsmen were reviewed, and in this situation, we sent out the call for two more doctors. The steadily increasing beat of the choppers alerted us to their arrival, and the helicopters settled down on the airstrip nearby. The ambulances were quickly back, and each patient was carried in to be initially surrounded by corpsmen and a doctor (or more, depending on the case). Those with relatively minor wounds were quickly checked and then freshly bandaged. Three of the first group had serious wounds, two possibly fatal. One Marine was blue and barely breathing from a neck wound. He got a fast tracheostomy (opening in the trachea or windpipe). At first it appeared we were going to be too late, but in a short time he looked better and was breathing again on his own. Both of the others were

118

shocky but conscious, one with multiple shrapnel wounds of his upper body, some severe burned areas, and traumatic amputations of both feet. Crude belt tourniquets had been placed around both lower legs. Dirty, bloody clothing was rapidly cut off, and vital signs were checked. He swore as both arms were quickly grabbed and IVs were started. I leaned over him, and much to my surprise I heard, "I know the feet are gone, Doc, but are the family jewels still there?"

The other Marine was pale, damp, and soaked with blood from a large abdominal wound from which loops of bowel had escaped. Both legs were fractured and deformed. The timely analgesia of shock and morphine allowed us to splint his legs and apply a large dressing to his gaping abdominal wound. We got IVs going with difficulty, because his veins were flattened and elusive. He lay quietly with an occasional soft curse, but his eyes were alert and still displayed sparks of fight and determination that could often be seen in even the hopelessly wounded.

Shouts of "fixed wing ready to go" were heard, and the serious cases were loaded into ambulances with an accompanying corpsman as an IV stand and attendant. These would go to A-Med today and would be on the operating table within 30 to 45 minutes. The destination varied, depending on the number of casualties, but included also the *Repose* and Da Nang. All three would probably make it, which was a tribute to the speed and refinement of the system developed here. We shipped them all out just in time to receive another load. These Marines were just about all KIAs — some of them had massive chest and head wounds. As I looked at one Marine near the front of the tent, a TV cameraman stepped inside. We swore loudly at him, and he was bodily thrown out. The insensitivity of some of the media at times was just unbelievable. This particular individual had already been told once to stay out of our way. Garber and I worked desperately on a very shocky young corpsman with a chest wound. He whispered to me that he couldn't breathe. We just couldn't get anything down fast enough, and he died tragically in front of us a few minutes later.

Then, as suddenly as it began, the onslaught ended, and attention was turned to cleaning up the resulting shambles of dirty battle dressings, bloody clothing, tape, needles, and assorted bandage materials. I made the sad trip over to Graves Registration to sign out the dead. It was a miserable job to say the least. There were 18—all young, all very much alive this morning, and now suddenly gone.

Back in the tent, Garber and I slumped down, drained and depressed. "Boy, does war ever suck or what," he said, shaking his head. The impact of these moments tended to wear off a little as we concentrated on those men we were able to help. Originally I had thought I was somewhat accustomed to taking care of major trauma cases after spending two months of my internship in the emergency room. But I soon discovered that the worst days in the ER were relatively minor league compared to dealing with the savage effects of modern weaponry on the human body. Even after eleven months of it, there was no getting hardened to the devastating sights. You just had to put yourself on a kind of numb automatic pilot and do the best that you could under the circumstances.

Later we sneaked into the official briefing and heard that a company of 1/26 had run into an ambush with small arms and mortar fire. Our casualties ran to 21 WIA and 18 KIA, but at least by all indications, the NVA really took their lumps. Some of the walking wounded said there were bodies all over the place, and an air officer reported observing 40 to 50 bodies with many additional probables by air and artillery strikes. After dinner on a cool quiet evening, we sat around in front of Garber's hootch listening to the distant boom of B-52 strikes. Nobody had much to say. It had turned out to be a bloody, long, and sad first day at Khe Sanh.

The following day was grey and misty with occasional brief rain. We spent part of the morning working on the hootch Hilton, which was amazingly dry with no leaks from above. However, gusts of wind blew water through the cracks in the wall, so we did some caulking with cotton and cast plaster. Garber, who was one year into his orthopedic residency when he was drafted, enjoyed the chance to get his hands in some plaster. Around 11 o'clock we treated one casualty who had one of those stories that verged on the miraculous. A Huey had taken some .50 calibre fire and had just barely made it back. The pilot had received instantaneous fatal wounds, and the co-pilot had done some fancy flying to land the damaged ship. Our patient was the co-pilot. His emergency takeover and successful landing became more incredible when we saw that his left hand had been completely blown off. His stump was only oozing and his vital signs were stable so he was not in any danger. "Flew that S.O.B. down with one hand," he kept repeating over and over as we cleaned and dressed his wound. Later we learned from some of the pilots that flying a Huey with one hand in spite of enemy fire, a disabled chopper, and the shock of his own wound, was a near-impossible feat.

A little later we were sitting around the tent, Garber in his shorts, when one of the corpsmen rushed in and told us that General Westmoreland was up at triage. Naturally this announcement resulted in some skeptical remarks. "No sh—, sir, I kid you not," persisted the corpsman. Garber stuck his head outside the tent and returned with eyes a little wide. "I'll be damned," he muttered as he began a record-breaking clothes-changing effort. I at least had on my utility trousers and boots, so I grabbed my shirt and got up there first. Sure enough, it was none other than the number-one man himself who came striding out of the triage tent where I hoped the duty corpsman was not asleep on a stretcher. His group included a whole parade of Marine Corps VIPs—General Cushman (three stars), General Hochmuth (two stars), and General Metzger (a mere one star). I really didn't notice them too much, with the famous face and four big stars scrutinizing me. Fortunately I managed to remember to salute. Then we shook hands, and it was all business as he proceeded to ask several questions about the co-pilot. He fit well the image of an experienced, competent professional soldier with his piercing gaze and bristling black eyebrows. About that time Garber made his appearance, and the General asked him more of the same questions. He was surprisingly quite specific in his questioning. "Was he in shock? Did you give him blood?" etc. Appearing satisfied with our answers, if not with our military appearance, he said "Thank you gentlemen," and was off, trailing generals and colonels behind him.

"Garber," I said, "how come you didn't ask him to inspect your hootch? Maybe he would have liked to join us for some coffee and pound cake." Garber didn't crack a smile and replied, "No way. He's got to make a reservation like everybody else."

Five days later I had my first chance for some sightseeing. The nature of our official business was to visit a missionary couple who lived near Khe Sanh. The wife was expecting to give birth soon, and we'd been asked to help out with some arrangements for transportation to Da Nang. Our expeditionary group consisted of two doctors, one corpsman, and a security force of two Marines. I had hopes of adding to our weapons arsenal by picking up a Bru crossbow. We left the plateau and dropped down into a gentle valley that was lush and green. It was a ten-minute drive to Khe Sanh, which was just a short distance west on Route 9 after leaving the narrow rutted road down from the base. Instead of the rural lowland setting to which I was accustomed, here we were in the midst of tall palms, coffee trees, brilliant red flowers, and dense vegetation threatening to overgrow the road in places. Dean Gentry, the corpsman with us, said there were supposed to be several old French coffee and rubber plantations around here that were still run by their original owners.

Khe Sanh, small and ramshackle at best, was populated mainly by lowland Vietnamese. The Montagnard villages were scattered through the surrounding hills away from Route 9. The locals seemed to be doing a fairly brisk business of selling crossbows and baskets, which I'm sure they got for practically nothing from the Bru. In addition, there were some less-than-authentic imitations made out of ammo boxes for the less discriminating. We stopped at an exceptionally well-supplied small dispensary run by an intense Special Forces medic with the help of two Vietnamese and a missionary nurse. Garber saw one of his Montagnard patients there, an elderly gentlemen who'd been brought up to the base with some shrapnel wounds of the leg which had become infected. The wounds looked good now, and the man, who had been nicknamed Louie-Louie as that was the best anybody could do with his real name, was effusive in his gratitude.

Through one of the Vietnamese who did the interpreting, Grant told him that he could easily repay him for his services with a few banana trees for his front yard. Louie-Louie seemed to understand, and, gesturing emphatically, he assured us that he would bring some. He still needed a crutch to get around, and he hobbled off, waving goodbye several times. Before we left, we saw a few other patients, including two men who looked like they'd had tuberculosis from the Year One. However, the medic told us that because of their rugged mountain environment, the Bru people were surprisingly healthy, without as much of the infectious and parasitic diseases that plagued the lowlanders.

From Khe Sanh we drove up a twisting, bumpy road to a renovated plantation house built against the side of the hill. Two fair-haired, blue-eyed children were playing outside with two very dark Montagnard youngsters. It could have been a United Nations poster scene. How could we possibly be a short distance away from a violent wartime existence? The Millers, a husband and wife team in their late twenties, belonged to a Bible-translating organization. Their goal was to translate the scriptures into the native language of primitive peoples, and at the same time teach them to read and write. Of course just to make it interesting, the Bru, like many such people, had no written language tradition at all. As a result, the Millers' first task was to learn the Bru tongue and then develop a written form.

It all sounded pretty overwhelming to me, but their organization was very active, with 17 other teams doing the same thing up and down the mountains of Vietnam. Mr. Miller said that all it required was a commitment to do God's work, lots of patience, and a good tape recorder. They had already been there over a year and a half and had recently moved to this house after spending the earlier time living in a Bru village. Usually each team would spend approximately five years in each area. It was certainly a long way from the near anonymity of the names of missionaries seen in a church bulletin. To see their dedication and faith in action was really an inspiration, and they both seemed quite happy and unconcerned about the war swirling around them.

We had an excellent meal of rice, chicken, and vegetables prepared by their Vietnamese housekeeper. Mr. Miller told us that in some areas the Montagnards liked to eat monkey but were reluctant to go out and hunt them because of the VC in the vicinity. Here the Communists had not bothered the Montagnards too much, possibly because they were all mainforce NVA. In regions in the South, the tribespeople had been forced to leave their villages and live as refugees in armed camps run by Army Special Forces units. I asked him what the reaction had been so far to the concept of Christianity. He smiled and said that he and his wife were optimistic about their prospects and really loved working with the Bru people. Amazing, I thought, as he described their basic animistic religious beliefs with elaborate rituals of sacrifice to pacify evil ancestor spirits. Mrs. Miller was about one month away from a visit from the stork, and we went over the possibilities for her obstetrical care in either Quang Tri or Da Nang. It turned out that she'd also had Rh problems in the past, so it really looked like Da Nang was the best choice.

At their suggestion we then went to visit the village where they had lived. Parking the jeeps, we hiked up a short trail to a small group of sturdy houses built on stilts three to four feet off the ground. The roofs were made of a thick, dense fibrous thatch with walls of woven bamboo. In front of some houses were tobacco leaves strung up to cure and large, flat round trays of coffee beans. Two bare-breasted women passed us carrying big wicker baskets filled with vegetables, and a small, dark wiry man sat impassively outside his house smoking a thin pipe with a tiny silver bowl. They did not seem too shocked to see some tall Americans, and a small group of children quickly surrounded us with the customary antics when my camera made its appearance. This time however, we had some additional entertainment. It was showtime thanks to Gentry, who had brought along a few magic tricks from his repertoire. Naturally, like children anywhere, the Bru youngsters were fascinated, and Gentry was a huge hit. They ran off happily, a few lucky ones with paper hats and flowers, and we walked back down the trail in great spirits. We didn't know a single word of their language and came from light years away in terms of cultural background, but yet we got along so easily. It was a moment to reflect on the total senselessness of war as a way to solve the problems of the world.

That night we sat out in front of Garber's hootch in the warm early evening hours like southern gentlemen sipping mint juleps on the veranda. In this case though it was more like coffee, tea and C-ration pound cake, but still it was a pleasant and relaxing end to an enjoyable day. The horizon would occasionally brighten slightly to the tune of the muffled boom of B-52s at work. Tall tales and reminiscing went on into the night until finally another hootch session began to break up. It all ended too abruptly on this particular evening because of a couple of casualties from some perimeter grenades. The blinking red lights of the medevac chopper brought back memories of my arrival in the darkness of another Khe Sanh night almost a week ago.

The following two days were marked by a lot of loafing in the sun and, fortunately, not much business in the triage tent for a change. Things had been pretty quiet without much contact out in the field. Actually we did fill a few sandbags, but as far as Garber's hootch was concerned, the big news was the return of Louie-Louie. We had definitely under-estimated our friend, because all of a sudden there he was with a big smile and a gunny sack containing three small banana trees. Our perimeter and tight security precautions apparently presented no real problem to a man with Louie-Louie's talents. Garber claimed that the fame of his hootch had spread even to the Marines manning the checkpoint on the road. With no pigs to sacrifice for the occasion, we had to settle for pouring some C-ration ham and lima beans in each planting hole.

Louie-Louie watched the whole landscaping ceremony with great curiosity. "Look at that," exulted Garber, "He's speechless. There's just no appropriate words in any language to describe my plantation."

"Could be," I replied. "On the other hand, after seeing you in action, he may be thinking how lucky he is that his leg is getting better."

"Gentry," shouted Grant, "get me an ambulance to give my honored guest a ride to the gate before he gets accidently zapped."

"You're a good man, Louie-Louie," he said, patting him on the back. "Take care of that leg."

"*Merci beaucoup,*" I added, grabbing his hand and shaking it. Louie-Louie smiled delightedly and saluted us as he turned to go. No doubt he would go back to his village tonight and talk about the strange Americans who could build flying machines, jeeps, and guns but couldn't figure out how to construct a decent house.

Later in the afternoon I walked over to the airstrip to finish off a roll of movie film. Believe it or not, I decided against more helicopter footage. Instead I planned on a shot of a C-130 roaring down the runway toward the camera. Positioning myself off to the side of the anticipated flight path, I readied myself for another academy-award-winning sequence as the transport's four engines reached a high-pitched scream. I changed the film speed to 12 ft/sec to accentuate velocity and zoomed closer so that the plane would fill most of the frame. As it approached me, all of a sudden it appeared to be headed almost straight at me. I decided it was a good time to get out of the way, but in the process I managed to trip on the metal grating and toppled over backwards. As I went down, I thought of the absurdity of being run over by our own plane with only a few weeks to go. I cringed as the monster thundered past and missed me by a comfortable margin. As I picked myself up, I realized I had been fooled by the foreshortened view, as the plane was actually a lot further away than it had looked. This great cinematographic performance had been seen by some Marines who were off-loading ammunition from some pallets nearby. I received a chorus of hoots and a voice called out, "Way to hang in there, Doc." I beat a fast retreat to the triage tent to get some first aid for my bruised ego.

That night we surprised the Marine officer corps by showing up at the official briefing. As usual, there were some impressive figures thrown at us by the air officer with regard to tons of ordinance dropped during the preceding 24 hours, including the nightly B-52 raid.

"Sounds a little expensive, doesn't it," I said leaning over to Grant. He nodded in reply, "Can't believe anything could survive that kind of blitz, except for my hootch of course."

We heard about reports of increased activity on the Ho Chi Minh Trail with possible sightings of tanks. The speculation was that we could expect more rocket attacks like the last one just prior to my arrival, which apparently had been aimed at the fuel depots. After that reassuring comment, we decided to check out the command bunker on the way back. It was dank and musty, but very solid, with massive heavy beams supporting the sandbagged roof.

"Nobody's going to get a tan in here, that's for sure," remarked Garber. I remembered spending some time in a similar bunker down at Dong Ha during a rocket attack. The rush for cover had almost been a stampede, and there were actually some requests for purple hearts from injuries sustained while falling down in the process. I had no desire to hear again the whine of those incoming rounds. That particular attack didn't last more than 30 minutes or so, and I recalled wondering how anybody could have possibly held up under the constant terror from the sky in Britain and other places during World War II. This bunker at Khe Sanh and many others there were to play a vital role in the survival of many Marines in months to come when the base was subjected to constant shelling during the 77-day siege which began in January of the following year.

The next day's first C-130 from Da Nang brought back the prodigal son. George had such a good time that he decided the least he could do was invest around $1200 in the local economy. His Bangkok bargains ran the gamut from star sapphires and bronzeware to some other interesting items like a leopard skin that was a steal at $100. Larry West had also come up from A-Med in the same plane. There were some plans to expand our medical capabilities, and he was going to spend a few days at Khe Sanh to assess the situation. Now all I needed was some transportation, and I was on my way. Garber also decided he'd go back to Phu Bai for a short change of pace since we had medical officers to spare at the moment. Actually, Larry came at the right time because that afternoon brought us one terrible casualty from an encounter with a "Bouncing Betty" type mine. This Marine would end up a triple amputee if he survived. We gave him all the blood we had on hand and sent him off to Phu Bai along with several others from Hill 881. Larry said that there was a new orthopod on call there today. What a way to start!

That night we had a classic hootch session that ended only when we were driven to cover by a genuine thunderstorm, featuring some good-sized raindrops plus some impressive lightning bolts up in the hills as well. The next morning we got some harrowing eye-witness accounts from the boys at the radio relay station up on Hill 950. Some of the strikes detonated about half of the claymore mines in the area. Fortunately, there was only one man with serious wounds, but there were a lot of bad headaches and ringing ears. The worst casualty looked like he'd been on the wrong end of a shotgun blast as he was peppered from head to foot with small pieces of shrapnel. All of these were not from a claymore but from a grenade that was lying underneath a flak jacket. Somehow it was detonated, riddling the vest, which nevertheless saved that Marine's life. The best story was about one man dressed only in his shorts who was seen holding his radio in a hole half-filled with water, a human lightning rod, if there ever was one, who ended up with only a headache.

Later Garber and I went over to the airstrip looking for our ride to Phu Bai. We expected a routine transport or helicopter ride sooner or later. However the day wore on, and it became apparent that space was at a premium and that we'd better start getting lucky or else a trip south was not going to be part of the day's agenda. We finally got our chance, but it wasn't exactly first-class transportation. The Army had a few weird, old ungainly, combination cargo-passenger planes called Caribous. I'd watched them struggle to take off a few times before, looking like some strange awkward bird that was learning to fly. It boiled down to a Caribou or bust for that day, so feeling adventurous, we grabbed a seat and hung on. Our luxury superjet rattled and shook but somehow got off the ground, leaving the green jungled terrain of Khe Sanh slowly behind. I caught glimpses of waterfalls and pools between towering trees. It was country that was surely meant for other things than to be subjected to rockets, artillery, and tons of B52 ordinance. What a site for a beautiful mountain retreat, I thought, as I concentrated on the scenery and not the peeling paint and loose rivets of the plane's interior.

After a brief stop at Quang Tri to pick up some passengers, it was another hold-your-breath take-off from a bumpy dirt runway.

Soon we bounced down at Phu Bai and lurched to a stop. We had returned in a little less style than when I left. I told Garber that if he was really lucky maybe there'd be another Caribou around for him to ride back up. How nice it would be to some day take a leisurely drive up Route 9 armed with only a camera and the pleasant anticipation of a hiking or exploring trip to the hidden streams and cool valleys in the hill country around Khe Sanh. For now though, that mountain plateau awaited its destiny as one of the storied names in the history of the Vietnam war.

Triage tent. Khe Sanh.

Montagnard boy in village near Khe Sanh.

Garber defending his hootch.

A small shot of Kaopectate.
Anti-Uncle Ho's revenge treatment.

Montagnards at Khe Sanh triage tent.

CHAPTER NINE

Fini Vietnam?

It wasn't long before I was back at the Phu Bai airport waiting for my last ride down to Da Nang. The remaining days were filled with long, jaunty bull sessions, and some good-byes to people and places that had played big parts in our lives during the past year. Sandy returned from his stint with the grunts, and he joined the rest of the A-Med short-timers for the stretch run. The sobering work of casualty cases continued with some heavy action taking place near the DMZ. Part of the time was spent taking care of one last project.

I returned from Khe Sanh to find a huge pile of small packages waiting in my hootch. The results of my mother's clothing drive, Operation Big Doc, had finally caught up with me. The clothes had come piecemeal in small shipments because large quantities all at once were too expensive by air and too slow by sea. She had done a terrific promotional and organizational job, and the articles were all sorted and ready to go. As we made our last visits to Hue and the junk fleet, we distributed the clothes along with our soap and medical items.

The final days passed quickly as we were cast adrift in Da Nang with our memories and loose ends. Sandy and I made the rounds of our familiar haunts with unexpected nostalgia. We ate crab and *pho* at a cafe on the river as we watched the polyglot collection of boats pass by. We actually spent some time one afternoon taking each other's incongruous picture "hunkering down" (squatting Asian style) on a busy street corner. Sandy had a girlfriend to visit, allegedly the possessor of the biggest boobs in I Corps. It was now our turn to sit at night telling war stories while wide-eyed newcomers tried to act nonchalant.

And then, early one morning, we were sitting in a 707 watching the airfield lights start to pick up speed. The plane lifted off, and there were scattered cheers. The long-awaited moment turned out to be quite a letdown for me—even a strange kind of sadness. Sandy and I both seemed to know that part of it was the knowledge that the excitement and intensity of living fairly close to the edge would be gone. In addition, I was surprised to find strong feelings of somehow running out on a job where I was really needed and leaving friends in trouble behind. It was Dai Loc all over again, only this time it was really over. Now it was even more clear why the degree of emotional involvement in some individuals led as far as extension of tours of duty in spite of all the hazards.

Sandy looked at me and shrugged, "Well *bac-si*, they're going to have to get along without us for awhile." I nodded as the plane climbed higher out over the South China Sea and headed back toward another world.

Upon returning home, I was immediately struck by the overwhelming affluence of a society that I had once accepted as the status quo. Compared to the world of the Vietnamese peasant, the average American family was living a life of luxury where material wealth and conveniences were in evidence everywhere. Medical care was so readily available. Need a *bac-si*? No problem—the yellow pages were virtually bursting with physicians from whom to choose. It was really a little disturbing to read and hear of the relatively minor concerns confronting many Americans in contrast to the majority of Vietnamese, who had more pressing problems than complaining about traffic, selecting a good TV program or picking a restaurant. And, yet, in spite of living in a situation where each day could bring terror and tragedy, where life-threatening disease was frequent, and where daily existence required extremes of manual labor, most Vietnamese country people remained warm and cheerful individuals who made the best of their war-ravaged existence. Of course, war or no war, most of them knew no other kind of life. But yet I had to fight off a pervasive feeling of distance from some of my fellow citizens who appeared somewhat shallow and decadent in comparison.

Questions came from friends and relatives about Vietnam and the war. At first I tried to answer carefully and convey some idea about what I experienced. But like many others, I soon had the feeling that there was no way I was going to be able to communicate the complex reality of Vietnam to my questioners. My enthusiasm for countering some distorted media-based ideas about Indochina with some of my own views gradually faded into a state of withdrawal from the subject entirely.

Nine months later, I received the first of several letters from Hoang Hai and the sequel to the Hue cathedral episode unfolded. Her father had received more threats, and he decided to take the family to stay with friends in Da Nang for awhile. They returned to Hue later in the year when the school term began. Her description of the events to follow during Tet and afterwards vividly tell the story.

March 1968, Da Nang

... You will be happy to receive my letter and it will make you don't be worry about me when you know VC attack and occupy my city for a month and there are 8,000 people dead at Hue...I stayed thirteen days under bunker. Every day I only eat a piece of pudding cake and drink a half a glass of water. Then US come to Hue to aid MACV compound and plane called everybody live near MACV have to leave home by two minutes because Americans will bomb my place and shoot cannon. I was too afraid, all my family get out of house and follow Americans to come to the University to stay there. We left house without luggage, food, money and about three days later, Marines let us go home because my place was liberated. We went home, but my house was destroyed and we lost everything. NVA soldiers stole all our clothes, moneys, rice, everything. My parents couldn't keep their tears, they are too moved. This is the second time they lost everything since in 1956 we immigrate from north to Hue...

April 1968, Da Nang.

...Do you know the German doctors at Hue? Doctor Krailick and Dr. Dissher. VC buried three German doctors and Dr. Krailick's wife. That was sad news for medical school. Three of them are my brother's teachers. They helped Vietnamese people. Medicine students organized the big funeral for them and many students couldn't keep out their tears when they attended the mass...

June 1968, Hue.

...It's still quiet, no rocket and mortar come down. I was happy to go back to my lovely city. Hue still is charming and attractive. Everything has changed, even heart of people here. Now after offensive they anti-VC. Most students despise them and enjoy their military training. Next week I have attend ambulance class too at the hospital...

The years passed and the war began to wind down. Once, three years after I left, I saw a short newspaper dispatch about a large NVA-VC assault on the village of Dai Loc that was beaten back by local militia and

ARVN troops. I felt a real surge of pride as I was quickly transported back over the Song Vu Gia river bridge into Dai Loc. At least in one place we may have succeeded in helping the Vietnamese develop the resources to help themselves. But overall, there seemed to be too much corruption, political infighting, and inadequate outside help with the eventual conclusion being the sad spectacle of the final withdrawal of 1974.

Wrestling with the same issues about the war is still not much easier now than in 1966-1967. Many people, of course, believe that the whole war effort was a terrible mistake. Especially among the media corps, it is a foregone conclusion that their self-righteous efforts to expose the mistakes, cover-ups, and fumbling of our military establishment were well justified and instrumental in bringing the war to an end. Nevertheless, I can personally testify that media accounts even by well-respected correspondents regarding events or places I knew well were sometimes distorted to the point of almost being unrecognizable. An unbiased report was altogether too infrequent, and there were a lot of liberal axes to grind. Thanks largely to this kind of coverage, public support for the war deteriorated, and even the 1968 Tet offensive, which was in fact a devastating military defeat for the Communists, resulted in a major psychological victory for the enemy.

However from our present vantage point, we are provided with a certain amount of historical perspective. The argument that was once put forth regarding the great strategic importance of Indochina and the domino theory can now be laid to rest without much difficulty. However if we look again at one of the major objectives leading to involvement in Vietnam, at what might now be referred to as the human-rights issue, we would still have to wonder if such a goal was not a worthwhile reason for some commitment after all, especially in the framework of the world of the sixties. At that time, President Kennedy's words were still fresh in our minds when he said that our country would "bear any burden, meet any hardship, support any friend, and oppose any foe to assure the survival and success of liberty." Unfortunately that ideological goal fell victim not to a battlefield defeat but to a combination of political, diplomatic, and psychological factors.

On a personal level as I have mentioned, when exposed firsthand to Communist tactics, it became very easy to become caught up alongside my Vietnamese friends with an overpowering desire to do anything possible to exterminate an oppressive enemy. They were not a shadowy abstraction as seen by the Vietnamese peasant but a raw real force in their village life. Once Americans had to fight for freedom that naturally at this point is taken for granted. How quickly we can lose sight of an

136

existence without the rights that we assume are as basic or automatic as breathing. Even in a country where sometimes an assault on a city street is ignored, I think most Americans would have risen up in outrage if confronted with the abuses inflicted on the Vietnamese in cold, calculated strategic attempts to intimidate and control the local population. But yet it is clear that we can't reverse all the world's inequities at the expense of our youth.

The question that always begged for an answer was, how could the Communists possibly do such things to their own people? The official line now is that most of the bombings, assassinations, and other deliberate terroristic tactics either never happened or were only directed against a few "criminals." Was a man like Father Matthieu such a criminal? Even the mass executions at Hue are largely denied or blamed on the "puppet" troops. My Lai notwithstanding, most of our so-called atrocities were more the unfortunate accidental variety—the errant artillery round, civilians caught in free-fire zones, and other tragic occurrences that so often occur to innocent people trying to keep out of the way of war. At least in 1966-1967, we seemed to take great pains to avoid such incidents most of the time, even at the expense of the effectiveness of our military operations. And when the inadvertent accident did occur, we did everything possible to help the victims. In stark contrast the Communists made no such attempts. Those patriots preferred to throw grenades into restaurants, blow up ambulances and buses, and bomb hospitals, as John Steinbeck once wrote in a dispatch from the delta region. "The VC invariably washed themselves with innocents...knowing our reluctance to return fire at the cost of people."

In recent years life in Vietnam under the Communist regime has not been just a relative inconvenience due to a differing political ideology. People driven to the point of gambling on any kind of leaky, overcrowded escape craft are not good evidence for a very reasonable way of life. Wholesale abandonment of possessions and sometimes family for the tenuous hope of a new life would testify to the fact that many Vietnamese were willing to risk everything to escape a situation in their homeland that must be intolerable.

If our political climate had allowed us to muster more military clout at the appropriate time, we might not have had to watch these people throw themselves to the perils of the open sea and the vagaries of unfriendly foreign governments. Having moved to Hawaii in 1973, I became a first-hand observer of a steady stream of fortunate Vietnamese who managed to leave successfully and were able to find sponsorship. Some of their stories were of incredible hardship, separated families, and personal tragedy. Many arrived with very little and spoke no English. It was not unusual to see former professional people washing dishes and doing janitorial work as they struggled to start over. Some ended up on welfare rolls, but a much larger number became self-sufficient and successful in an amazingly short time. With the traditional emphasis placed on education, many of the children soon excelled in school. A young Vietnamese girl was picked by President Reagan to give her simple, moving speech during the Statue of Liberty celebration. Her story was typical, going from no knowledge of English to being one of the spokespersons for all Americans on the meaning of freedom and liberty. How eloquently such individuals can remind us of how very fortunate we all are.

Nevertheless, although many of our Vietnamese Americans have become model citizens, the fact remains that they were forced to leave their homeland, some under desperate circumstances. Could it all have been avoided? Could all the self-torment and soul-searching of the American conscience as well as the need to swallow a military defeat have been erased? An ARVN surgeon in Hue who had once fought for the Viet Minh against the French told me that the only way for the Americans to stop the Communists was to invade the north, or at least mount an attack on the Ho Chi Minh trail. He couldn't seem to understand why our government was so timid when we had such great strength at our disposal. The Communists' big hope, he said, was that our vocal press and our political situation would continue to paralyze us into relative inaction and enhance chances for a prolonged war of attrition in which the Americans would eventually lose interest. Other Vietnamese I knew also seemed to have almost a mystical faith in the great power of the wealthy U.S.A. They felt that if we really wanted to, we could simply crush the Communist forces like offending cockroaches.

Of course, in retrospect, the Communist strategy of attrition couldn't have worked much better. We will never know how the outcome would have been altered by a resolve to bring the war to a rapid conclusion with a more aggressive and unrestricted military campaign. The often heard complaint and consequences of having to "fight with one hand tied behind our back" would have been absent. It is tempting to speculate that perhaps many lives would have been saved on both sides, and America's self-image and esteem would not have suffered such a major blow.

At the present time, the economic situation in Vietnam has worsened to the point where some restructuring of basic Marxist tenets has been undertaken. The thorn in the ideological side, Ho Chi Minh City, never really lost its free enterprise leanings and now such an approach may even be receiving cautious official encouragement throughout much of the country. A concomitant gradual change in the traditional hard-core older leadership is occurring. The Vietnamese have become disenchanted with their Soviet allies and to be Russian is to be tolerated or even in some quarters to be the subject of an almost palpable contempt. In contrast, and in spite of the past, American sins seem to have been largely forgiven and interest in our rock stars, our movies, our clothes, and all aspects of our culture continues to grow. Pursuit of the American dollar is also developing. The cycle has come around to the current solicitation of American tourists for a different kind of tour in Vietnam.

The sun was warm on my back as I looked at the familiar long black wall. It was a fine bright morning in Hawaii, and there was an occasional rustle of coconut palm fronds overhead. The replica, which was about two-thirds the size of the original memorial, had been in Honolulu several days as part of a veterans' organization's country-wide tour. Many visitors had come already. The wall was draped with leis, and at its base were bunches of cut flowers, orchids, and anthuriums as well as some burnt down candles. There were pictures and other mementos, and a few notes with poignant messages were taped to the wall.

The outpouring of aloha visible here was much different than the austerity that surrounded my visit to the real memorial on a cold crystalline Washington morning three years ago. There I looked for specific names and stood for a long time, feeling the intense emotions evoked by that stark black marble wall. Sweatsuited joggers and strolling tourists seemed to pass by unconcerned, as if the whole subject and the 58,000 names didn't really exist. Here though, I didn't feel that sense of isolation. It was as though it was all right for people to express their feelings openly and say: Yes, we know you suffered and sacrificed, and we will not forget.

I walked away slowly thinking of the morning that I left A-Med. I was walking across the road to the terminal. There was a lively eight-year-old boy nicknamed Shrimp, who had been semi-adopted by some of the Marines in the motor pool. We had introduced him to baseball, and some-body had found him an LA Dodgers cap. He ran up to me and saw my bag.

"Fini Vietnam, Bac-si ?" he said.

I nodded down at him and replied, *"Toi di ve"* (I am going), but then shaking my head, I continued, "but not fini Vietnam."

He looked a little puzzled but laughed as I gave him my best Marine salute. He snapped to attention and saluted back, knocking his cap sideways in the process.

Fini Vietnam?

Glossary

ARVN Army of Vietnam.

BAS Battalion Aid Station.

Bac-si Vietnamese word for doctor.

C-130 Large transport aircraft.

CAP Combined Action Platoon. Small unit consisting of a squad of Marines, one Navy corpsman, and local Vietnamese militia. Located in rural areas usually near a small village or hamlet.

Claymore mine Anti-personnel mine with a one pound charge of plastic explosive behind 600 small steel balls.

CO Commanding Officer.

CP Command Post.

Dai-uy Vietnamese word for Captain

DMZ Demilitarized Zone. Established along 17th parallel by 1954 Geneva accords.

FMSS Field Medical Service School.

Gook Derogatory term for Vietnamese or other Asians in past wars.

Grunt Slang term for a marine infantryman. Supposedly originated from the sound one made when picking up backpack.

GMO General Medical Officer. Usually a physician just out of internship with no specialty training.

hardback Frame wooden structure with corrugated metal roof and screened sides. Found in improved rear area unit locations.

hootch Slang term primarily for hardback.

Huey UH-lB helicopter gunship.

KIA Killed in Action.

LZ Landing Zone.

MEDCAP Medical Civil Affairs Program.

Medevac Medical evacuation usually by helicopter.

MACV Military Assistance Command Vietnam. Overseeing all of the various military units in Vietnam.

M14 Standard issue semi-automatic U.S. rifle later replaced by M16.

M16 After 1967, the standard American military weapon. Automatic/semi-automatic assault rifle.

NCO Non-Commissioned Officer.

NVA North Vietnamese Army.

NSA Naval Support Activity.

PFC Private First Class.

Popular Forces (PF) Local Vietnamese militia. Often poorly trained and not very reliable.

R & R Rest and Recreation—mainly outside of Vietnam, but also in-country sites as well. Most in demand: Hawaii for married individuals and Bangkok and Hong Kong for others.

RVN Republic of Vietnam.

Seabees Navy Mobile Construction Battalion.

2/4 Marine unit designation as in second battalion fourth Marine regiment.

USAID U.S. agency for international development.

USMC United States Marine Corps.

VC Viet Cong, derived from Vietnam Cong San (Vietnamese Communist). Also Victor Charlie or Charlie.

Vietminh Coalition founded by Ho Chi Minh that fought the French.

Ville Term for village. From French.

WIA Wounded in action.